WITHDRAWN

WORK FROM HOME

WORK FROM HOME

JUDY HEMINSLEY

howtobooks

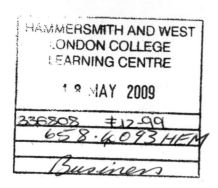
Published by How To Books Ltd,
Spring Hill House, Spring Hill Road,
Begbroke, Oxford OX5 1RX, United Kingdom
Tel: (01865) 375794 Fax: (01865) 379162
info@howtobooks.co.uk
www.howtobooks.co.uk

How To Books greatly reduce the carbon footprint of their books by sourcing their typesetting and printing in the UK.

British Library Cataloguing in Publication Data.
A catalogue record for this book is available from the British Library.

ISBN 978 1 84528 335 3

Produced for How To Books by Deer Park Productions, Tavistock
Typeset by PDQ Typesetting, Newcastle-under-Lyme, Staffordshire
Printed and bound by Cromwell Press Group Ltd, Trowbridge, Wiltshire

Every effort has been made to trace the copyright holders of material used in this book but if any have inadvertently been overlooked the publishers will be pleased to make the necessary arrangements at the first opportunity.

NOTE: The material contained in this book is set out in good faith for general guidance and no liability can be accepted for loss or expense incurred as a result of relying in particular circumstances on statements made in the book. The laws and regulations are complex and liable to change, and readers should check the current position with the relevant authorities before making personal arrangements.

CONTENTS

ACKNOWLEDGEMENTS

I am grateful to everyone who helped me to make this book possible and I would like to thank: Nigel Heminsley who inadvertently got me started on the homeworking path, Sara Barrett for all the cups of coffee and moral support, Susannah Marriott for her inspiring and thorough teaching, Ron Trewellard and Margaret Chamberlain for giving me useful feedback and boosting my confidence, and all the homeworkers who gave so generously of their time and experience in telling me their stories – I have not been able to mention them all but every one of you gave me vital information and inspiration.

And especially Andy Britnell, who kept up a constant supply of tea, toast and encouragement, and most importantly of all, who kept the faith.

INTRODUCTION

Are you one of the millions of people who have already discovered the rewards of working from home? Or one of those thinking about taking the plunge and wondering what challenges you will face? If so, this might be the book that will change your life. I have worked from home for nearly 20 years, so I'm well acquainted with all of its advantages and pitfalls. Over 12 years I started, built up and finally sold a very profitable cleaning business, which I ran from a spare bedroom. I have also worked from home as an employee, advising small businesses on development and obtaining finance. All I had to do was sit down at my desk, get out my timesheet and immediately I was earning!

There's a lot of my own experience in the pages of this book, but don't just take it from me. I've also spoken to many other homeworking pioneers who have already blazed the trail and have generously shared their experiences, good and bad. From designers to B&B owners, from sales managers to craftsmen, they have explained their solutions to common challenges that you might face. You will save time and aggravation by not having to make the same mistakes they did.

We have all encountered our fair share of joys and mishaps, and our ways of handling them may vary, but we all agree on one thing – we believe that the pros of homeworking far outweigh the cons and cannot imagine ever wanting to work any other way.

I can organise my day as it suits me. If I have a deadline, I can set my alarm early and start work in minutes. Or I can do the laundry or last night's washing-up before switching on my computer. If my energy or enthusiasm dip during the day, I go for a walk, have a nap or head out to do some errands. Sometimes I just don't get into the swing of things until the evening, and then I can work on until I'm ready to fall into bed.

I accept that there will inevitably be drawbacks - everyone I interviewed for this book mentioned dealing with issues like isolation, procrastination, and balancing work and family demands – but I still believe working from home is by far the best way to organise your life. It offers control and flexibility, saves time and fuel, and allows more time with friends and family. In other words, you have a far better quality of life when all your activities are centred around one location rather than two, or even more.

There are now estimated to be over 3 million people working from home in the UK, and the number is expected to rise steeply in the next few years. Given this, I decided to write a guide to working from home which can be used both by employees and by those who are self-employed. The defining factor here is not *who* pays your income, but *where* you earn it. Or as I read somewhere – work is what you do, not a place you go. Whether you run your own business or work for a large company, you will share experiences and be looking for solutions to similar challenges.

This is a down-to-earth, practical and friendly guide to getting the best from working from home. You won't find those irritating photographs of models sitting on white sofas and idly tapping laptops that often accompany homeworking stories in the media! The popular media image is far removed from real people's experience.

What you will find are true stories from the people who have balanced the working from home conundrum in their own unique ways and continue to do so. There are as many ways to do this as there are homeworkers, and the balancing act is ongoing. There are lots of options in this book to help you choose and develop the style which best suits you and your family. For example, many homeworkers need to have a door they can close to shut out distractions. Clayton, however, (see page 67) has discovered he much prefers to work in the living room where he is available to his young son. If this makes him fall behind with his work, he simply catches up in the evening when his son is in bed. Liam (page 83) uses ear plugs to keep out distracting sounds and help his concentration, whereas Robin puts on rousing music when he is starting to flag. Barry felt totally unable to work at home on his own and so took his laptop out to a local café with wi-fi (page 118). Completely different solutions, but they work for each individual.

Don't feel that you have to read the whole book from beginning to end, start with the bits that are most relevant to you now, and then dip in and out as you have the time and need. If you are pushed for time, you will find a summary of the main points at the start of each chapter, plus a list of useful resources at the end so you can start making changes straightaway.

Throughout the book I refer to the traditional workplace, the place you commute to, as the 'office'. This is simply because it is easier to choose a word and stick to it, not because I am excluding the many people who work in a shop, restaurant, factory, workshop, hotel, studio etc.

I hope you enjoy reading this book, and that it will help you to get the best out of working from home.

Judy Heminsley www.workfromhomewisdom.com

Part 1
Sounds like a Nice Idea

1
WHY WORK FROM HOME?

It was not so long ago that going off to work each morning was the accepted thing to do, and anyone who worked from home was the exception. Times have certainly changed. Since the Office for National Statistics started collecting data on the subject in 1997, the number of people working from home has trebled. In 2005, its Labour Market Trends survey found that 3.1 million people, or 11% of the UK workforce, were working from home full time, and many more for part of the working week. And, apparently, many office-bound workers aspire to do so.

> **It's a fact that...**
> In a survey carried out by insurance company Cornhill Direct in 2007, 69% of workers claimed they would work from home if they were given the choice. One in five were so keen to do so, they said they would even accept a pay cut.

Estimates of growth by 2012 vary from 22% of the workforce working from home to an astonishing 50% (predicted by Work Wise UK, which promotes smarter working practices). You may have considered homeworking yourself, and maybe you dismissed it as impossible, given your circumstances. But there are many reasons why working from home might improve your life, and all kinds of people manage to achieve it. This chapter aims to help you assess the realities of your own situation by reviewing the reasons so many people have already chosen home in preference to the office.

This chapter covers:

1. The reasons why more than 3 million people already work from home and why this number is set to rise sharply.

2. How you can work from home whether you are self-employed or working for someone else.

3. The advantages of working from home for you, for business, the community and the environment.

4. The downsides of homeworking – factors to consider carefully before making a decision.

5. A questionnaire to find out how prepared you are to become a homeworker and what kind of information will help you to gear up to homeworking.

My Story

Working from home was not something I ever planned to do; I just fell into it when my then husband's idea to clean the windows of large country houses evolved into a rapidly-growing contract cleaning business. We entertained the occasional sales rep. at the dining room table, where we also interviewed prospective staff. Deliveries of cleaning products arrived at the front door and our signwritten Suzuki jeep was parked in the street.

I ran the business from home for 12 years, building up my client base and finally selling it as a going concern. At my busiest times I employed over 20 people part time, and it was all entirely manageable from that bedroom base. Since then I've also worked from home as an employee and running other businesses. I'm now in my fifth home office and it feels entirely natural to be able to organise my whole life – including the shopping, washing, cleaning, visiting family and friends, going to the hairdresser, and so on – from one place, and not to have to jam all the so-called 'domestic' or 'personal' bits into the brief times between and after office hours.

I like the feeling that all these activities comprise my life, and that there is no artificial division between 'work' and 'home'. I suppose that's what we mean when we talk about work/life balance. I've worked in an office as well, but I much prefer working from home, and that's how I see myself in the future, whether I'm working for myself or someone else.

Why work from home?

Over three million British homeworkers and rising can't all be wrong, and the increase in numbers is not surprising when we look at all the diverse factors – economic, social and political – that are contributing towards fewer people travelling to a central place on a daily basis. Each homeworker has their own reasons, or combination of reasons, for making this choice. These range from the desire to lead a less stressful life and see more of their family to the need to cut the costs of transport at a time when housing and utility bills eat up more disposable income than ever before. Since so many more jobs can now be done remotely, it's no wonder that concerns about pollution and climate change are also leading people to choose homeworking. Let's look at each of these factors in turn.

USE THE TECHNOLOGY

The internet has allowed us to transfer information on a scale and at a speed never previously experienced. The advent of broadband has enabled huge files to be sent and received which previously would have required physical delivery. All kinds of jobs can now be done by people at home when before they would have needed to go to a library or company headquarters to access expert information. Sophisticated search engines mean we have access to experts wherever we are. Multinational companies can hold global meetings with videoconferencing and nobody has to get on a plane. Salesmen access up-to-date prices and stock levels on the company intranet before seeing clients, and submit orders online immediately afterwards. Mobile phones and Blackberries allow us to be in touch with colleagues all over the globe 24 hours a day. Run your own business, and with a professional website, no-one will know or even care where you are based. Problems with the computer you rely on? Remote access means that IT support can take a look and fix it from a distance. And when you want to save all that precious information, you can back it up remotely to make sure it's safe from fire, flood or theft and complies with statutory requirements.

A Journalist's Story

13 years ago Tim was a magazine editor in central London, coping with a stressful job, the pressures of city living and what appeared to be declining health. He was fortunate to be working for a forward-looking charity that agreed to let him work full time from home; an enlightened attitude at a time when homeworking was almost unheard of, the internet was in its infancy and there was no broadband. But he was able to take the opportunity to move out of London back to the rural area where he was born and in time, again with the consent of his enlightened employer and as the internet developed, to take on bits of freelance work, writing housing and regeneration reports. Eventually he gave up the job to become a freelance report writer. His business has grown in tandem with improvements in technology, particularly broadband, and he is now a specialist consultant in live/work schemes, subcontracting elements of his work to other self-employed professionals around the country, and working for clients all over the UK.

HAVE A BETTER WORK/LIFE BALANCE

Employees are fed up with wasting their precious work and leisure time in traffic queues and crowded trains when they could be at their desks or with their families. Daily commuting is tiring, stressful and expensive, and more and more people who are able to earn a living away from the major centres of commerce are moving out. Working from home gives you control over every aspect of your life, so you can forget about conforming to office culture and do your work the way you want, when you want. Ignore the phone ringing when you're concentrating and nobody will be glaring at you. You can fit in all the pieces of the jigsaw in the way that is most convenient to you. I can't imagine how I could possibly have run my life successfully over the last few years if I hadn't been working from home. I have had all kinds of commitments throughout the UK, sometimes at short notice, but somehow, with the freedom I have in my working life, it's all worked out and everything gets done.

A Webmaster's Story

Inspired by the recent birth of her daughter and her love of the outdoors, Clare recently moved to the country from Birmingham. With her husband, she runs a website enabling teachers to find destinations for school trips. 'The environment is cleaner and the way of life is more laid back. People here are easier going; people in cities are more stressed. I think the move has worked for me because I have reached a stage in my life where I want different things. I used to enjoy being part of a big office, and all the socialising. Now I'd rather be outside – I go running outside now, where I used to go running in the gym.' As their work can be done at any time of day, Clare and her husband work three days and two evenings a week, and use the other time to get out and explore the countryside.

SAVE MONEY

Let's face it, commuting today is extortionately expensive. If you drive your own car you have to pay for petrol and parking, possibly road tolls and the congestion charge, depending where you live. And don't even think about exceeding the time on your parking ticket or stopping on double yellow lines to pick up a pint of milk on the way home. If you use public transport you have to contend with ever-increasing fares for ever-more crowded services, delays and unexpected cancellations.

Just participating in office life costs money. You want to fit in and not be thought standoffish or peculiar, so you go along for the coffees, the lunches and the drinks after work; maybe some meals and nights out as well. And you have to look the part, the smartly groomed professional by day, the fashionable party-goer by night. You need to have enough clothes to mix and match so you're not the sad one who wears the same thing day in, day out, and have you noticed that suits and 'office clothes' always need dry cleaning?

If you have children or want to start a family, you will know that the cost of nursery care has risen consistently over the last few years, at well above the rate of inflation. Put that alongside the recent well publicised scares over the quality of care and security at nurseries and parents are becoming reluctant to pay nursery fees. How much better to juggle your work to fit around naps, playgroups and bedtimes?

We are all well aware of the astronomical price of buying or renting property, and that includes commercial property. BT have found that for every member of staff who works from home, they save an average of £6000 per annum on office costs. And if you're self-employed, you probably wouldn't be in business if you had to pay a commercial rent. Many business plans just don't stack up if buying or renting commercial property is added in. Our cleaning business certainly wouldn't have got off the ground if we had had to run it from business premises, and even after it became profitable, I never considered moving it away from home.

HELP FIGHT CLIMATE CHANGE

A few years ago there was widespread concern about the 'food miles' involved in flying food from places like South America and Africa to British supermarkets. Since then there has been a noticeable rise in the popularity of farmers' markets and a strong emphasis on the promotion of local and seasonal produce.

But have you heard of 'work miles', or the distances clocked up by commuters travelling to and from their workplaces every day? If not, it may not be long before you do. In a world of congestion, pollution and high petrol prices, it's increasingly illogical for thousands of people to spend hours every working day slogging to and from a place of work if they can do that work just as effectively from home.

With unusual and extreme weather events now regularly occurring in the UK, such as the torrential rain that caused the summer floods of 2007, there is more public debate about the effects of climate change and how cutting down on carbon emissions from driving could help to halt or reverse the effects.

Just a thought

According to Liftshare, the organisation providing free carshare and transport information, if the average car commuter halved the daily 19 miles they drive in their own car, 648 kilograms of carbon dioxide – the amount that could be absorbed by 216 trees – would be saved every year.

In 2006 David Miliband, the then Secretary of State for Environment, Food and Rural Affairs, proposed the idea of personal carbon allowances or carbon credit cards. Consumers would have to carry a swipe card recording their carbon allowance, which would have points deducted each time they filled up with petrol or bought an airline ticket. Those not using their allowance could sell surplus points to a central bank, from which heavy users could buy more points. A feasibility study has recommended the scheme could come into use by 2012.

It's a fact that...

in order to ensure that the UK plays its part in tackling climate change the government needs to commit to reducing the country's carbon emissions by 80% in the new Climate Change Bill, and not the 60% that is currently on the table.

Source: WWF, 2007

CONSERVE OIL SUPPLIES

The western world has been founded on the availability of cheap oil and constant economic growth, so 'peak oil', when world oil supplies can no longer meet demand and start to decline, is a controversial and emotive subject. It is still refuted in some quarters, but even the International Energy Agency, which promotes affordable and reliable energy supplies for world consumers, announced in July 2007 that at some point in the not-so-distant future, probably by 2012, worldwide oil production will peak and then go into irreversible decline. It's mind-boggling to anticipate the impact this would have on our daily way of life.

It's a fact that...

the UK has one of the longest commutes in Europe. The average commuter travels for 58 minutes a day and one in ten people have a daily journey in excess of two hours. 'Extreme commuters', who commute at least three hours per day, make up 3% of the population.

Source: The RAC Foundation, 2007

If demand cannot be filled by supply, the law of basic economics will take over and the price of oil will shoot up. The most obvious and immediate effect could be that fuel would be rationed, as mentioned above, and that eventually driving would become too expensive for most people. It is vital we start to cut back on travel now and source more commodities locally in order to defer the peak oil crisis and set in motion the fundamental lifestyle changes which might be needed in the near future. Living and working in the same place might one day be a necessity rather than a choice.

Who can work from home?

Certain occupations lend themselves to homeworking because tasks are carried out primarily using the phone and computer equipment. Anybody in the IT industry has a head start on homeworking, as you can utilise your skills wherever you can carry and connect a computer. Sales and marketing roles are also easily carried out at home for similar reasons.

The latest development in call centres is enabling more people to work from home.

Originally call centres were run from a large, centralised location in the UK, while later 'offshoring' moved the work to countries like India where labour is much cheaper. Companies in industries that require staff to have detailed knowledge of their market are now 'homeshoring' and offering customer service positions to people at home in the UK who work flexible hours. Co-op Travel Group run the UK's largest 'virtual contact centre' and employ more than 600 staff, who work at home. Texperts' office is in the UK but they contract people living all over the world to answer the questions their customers send in by text.

SOME JOBS CAN'T BE DONE FROM HOME

Of course there are some jobs that just can't be done from home and never will. You can't work from home if you are a nurse, a lorry driver or a restaurant chef. It may be that there are materials and equipment kept at your place of work that can't be moved to your home. Or perhaps you need to be in regular face-to-face contact with colleagues and clients at your office.

But in some cases it may be perfectly possible to re-organise your working day in order to spend some time at home and the rest at the office or out with clients. Or you might put a new spin on your existing skills and practise them from home on a self-employed basis. A chef could cater for events from his home kitchen, or develop a range of meals for sale to retailers. The lorry driver could start up a courier business run from a spare room. In Chapter 3, we look at how to get started as a homeworker whether you need to negotiate homeworking with your boss or come up with a way to make money at home through self-employment or starting a small business.

What's so good about homeworking?

Sarah, a sales executive who works from home in a remote rural area, was so convinced that working from home was her best option that she persevered for a year, through many rejections and finally a gruelling three-hour interview, until she found an employer willing to give her a chance. Many of the people I spoke to while researching this book are equally enthusiastic about working from home. What exactly is it that we appreciate so much? Well, there are benefits not only for you as an individual, but also for businesses, for the community and the environment. Here are the advantages as I see them.

ADVANTAGES OF HOMEWORKING FOR YOU

- ☐ If you're an employee you save money on travelling, childcare, buying and drycleaning work clothes, on drinks, snacks and impulse shopping.

☐ You gain hours every day by not having to battle to the office and back. You can use that time to sleep in, get organised, play with the kids, do the cleaning or whatever suits you best.

☐ You can turn out more better quality work when you're not being distracted by colleagues and events in the office.

☐ Forget the stress of worrying about being stuck on public transport and arriving late, or of negotiating traffic jams and avoiding dangerous drivers on the motorway.

☐ You enjoy better work opportunities when you are not restricted to jobs within commuting distance – see Chapter 3 for how Sarah progressed from a low salary to being the family's main breadwinner by finding a job she could do from home. You can make a living or earn pocket money even if you are tied to the house and retain your job even if you move hundreds of miles away.

☐ You can design your own life. At home you have greater independence and flexibility. Nobody is going to tell you when to go for coffee and what time to get back from lunch. You can take work calls outside office hours, or personal calls in office hours, and work at the times you are naturally more productive.

☐ You can be at home when a delivery or workman is due to arrive 'any time between 9 a.m. and 5.30 p.m.' and take the first available appointment to see the doctor and dentist. Getting time off for the school play and sports day is no longer a problem. Time for community activities is a real possibility.

☐ And maybe you'll even become fitter, slimmer and healthier – no more tempting coffee shops and sandwich bars, no cream cakes on birthdays. Exercise can be slotted between tasks to benefit brain as well as body.

ADVANTAGES OF HOMEWORKING FOR BUSINESSES

☐ Property costs and overheads are reduced by not having to house so many staff. According to Work Wise UK, Microsoft has been encouraging flexible working for its staff and in so doing has managed to accommodate 400 more staff at its Reading headquarters. The building of new offices has already been postponed by two years, saving the company about £1 million a year.

☐ Small home-based businesses avoid expensive commercial rents and mortgages and the associated utility bills.

□ By showing themselves to be forward-thinking and open to innovation, employers attract highly qualified and highly motivated staff.

□ Employers find it easier to retain these high quality staff and save money on expensive recruitment and training.

□ All these savings enhance competitiveness in the face of tough competition from home and abroad.

ADVANTAGES OF HOMEWORKING FOR COMMUNITIES

□ You and your neighbours all benefit from the security of having someone in the house all or part of the day.

□ Your local area becomes more vibrant if people are around for the whole day and need to use local services. Homeworkers get their paper from the local newsagent and their stamps from the post office. Ideally they also have the time and inclination to do their food shopping locally too, enabling the survival of small food shops otherwise squeezed out by out-of-town superstores.

□ The roads get less congested at traditional rush hours. Think what a difference it makes to traffic flow when the schools are on holiday – how much quieter would the roads be if up to 50 per cent of the working population were working from home?

ADVANTAGES OF HOMEWORKING FOR THE ENVIRONMENT

Carbon emissions into the atmosphere are reduced as homeworkers:

□ Cut down their work miles.

□ Turn down the heating, get better insulation and switch off computers and appliances to keep utility bills down.

□ Shop locally and maybe grow their own fruit and vegetables in some of the time saved by not commuting.

The downsides of homeworking

It has to be said that there are those who are less than impressed by the idea of homeworking. In an article about public transport and the horrors of commuting in the *Daily Telegraph* in July 2007, Boris Johnson declared that 'the office is the natural habitat of Homo sapiens' and 'working from home is simply a euphemism for sloth, apathy, staring out of the window and random surfing of the internet'. I've also read a response to an internet article in which the writer declared that if you are able to work from home full time, you obviously have a useless job!

These outbursts are probably prompted by a wish to stir up controversy, but of course there's a price to be paid for everything and I'd rather we look at the potential pitfalls of homeworking at the outset. What's the price you pay for all these wonderful benefits of home working?

DISADVANTAGES OF HOMEWORKING FOR YOU

☐ When you work from home you lose your daily contact with colleagues and may begin to feel isolated. This side-effect of homeworking was mentioned by every one of the homeworkers I talked to when researching this book. Unless you are willing to accept that it's entirely your responsibility to work out your own way of dealing with feeling isolated and building a supportive network, then you are unlikely to be happy working from home.

☐ Being in closer contact with your family, on the other hand, might cause friction unless you can agree and adhere to workable boundaries.

☐ You may find it hard to create a productive structure for the working day.

☐ Spending all your time in one area may feel claustrophobic, and you might miss the stimulation of a change of scene, your colleagues, and shops and restaurants.

☐ It can be difficult to keep up the self-discipline required to maintain a steady pace of work when nobody else is around to see what you're doing.

☐ On the other hand, some people find it hard to switch off when work is so close at hand – you might become a workaholic addicted to your 'CrackBerry'.

DISADVANTAGES OF HOMEWORKING IF YOU ARE ALSO AN EMPLOYEE

☐ Office-based colleagues may be resentful of those working from home, seeing it as an unfair perk open to skiving, so that you find yourself working extra hard (skipping breaks and working long hours) just to prove that you are pulling your weight.

☐ Sometimes managers are opposed to the idea, fearing a fall in the quality and quantity of work produced.

A Marketing Manager's Story

Rachel works four days a week as a marketing manager and is one member of a team of homeworkers based throughout the country: 'If I'm in the middle of something and want to concentrate, I don't answer the phone. My bosses all work from home too and so they understand what it's like. If they were office based, it could be awkward, as they might suspect me of skiving.'

☐ Managers may regard home working as a perk which should be reserved for management, or fear for their own jobs as more and more staff work out of the office.

☐ You may get little support for the stresses of homeworking – internet and phone problems, feeling isolated, for example – when your colleagues are feeling like 'it's alright for some.'

☐ Team spirit might suffer if you are not all in the same place, so effective communications need to be set up to counter this, to share information and keep the consistency of your results.

☐ If you want promotion, you will have to work hard to stay at the forefront of the minds of those who make the decisions.

DISADVANTAGES OF HOMEWORKING IF YOU ARE SELF-EMPLOYED

☐ With no public presence, home-based businesses can be almost invisible, making it harder to get established and increase your market.

☐ Your detachment from commercial centres also means that your access to business information and advice will depend on how good you are at researching what is available in your area.

Is homeworking for me?

I hope that has given you an honest idea of the issues relating to homeworking. Without exception or prompting, all the homeworkers I spoke to mentioned that although there are pros and cons to working from home, they felt the pros far outnumbered the cons and they wouldn't want to work in any other way. The aim of this book is to maximise the advantages and help you minimise the drawbacks. Having read about them both, do you think working from home might be a choice you would make? And if so, how close are you to achieving it?

QUESTIONNAIRE – ARE YOU READY FOR HOMEWORKING YET?

Now you've weighed up all the reasons for working from home, its possibilities and its pitfalls, this questionnaire will help you to look carefully at your own circumstances, from your physical surroundings to your own skills and experience. If some do not immediately appear to be ideal, there may be ways to work on them to give you the best chance of success.

Think about each of the following statements and decide whether it is true or false for you. Answer as honestly as you can, not as you wish you were! Award yourself one point for each statement you believe is true for you, add up your overall score and read your assessment below.

☐ I already possess adequate skills to do my work successfully from home.

☐ My home is big enough to accommodate my work. (You do not necessarily have to have a spare room, but you do need to estimate just how much physical space is required.)

☐ My family understands and accepts my need for space and peace while I am working.

☐ I have the self-discipline required to keep up a steady stream of work.

☐ I am sufficiently experienced to be able to carry out my work without regular support from others.

☐ I accept the need to take responsibility for getting out and meeting people.

☐ I trust my family to adhere to the boundaries I set up with them regarding work and home life.

☐ I am willing to learn about myself, to accept my weaknesses, and to adapt my habits accordingly.

☐ I already have, or have confirmed it is possible to arrange, the facilities essential for my work (phone line, broadband connection, access to post box etc.).

☐ If you are employed: there is already a high level of mutual respect and trust between me and my manager.

☐ If you are self-employed: I have investigated the legal requirements of working from home e.g. council permissions, licences, insurance etc.

Your score:

0–3 It seems as though it's still early days to be thinking about working from home. Look closely at the statements that are not yet true for you. Is there anything here that you can start to work on? Perhaps you could start to develop your skills or plan to make changes to your home, even to move house. Go to Chapter 2 for more about the importance of personality and knowing yourself. Chapter 4 looks at the practicalities of adapting your home to accommodate your workspace.

4–7 You are well on the way towards homeworking but there is still work to be done. Try to identify the main areas you need to work on. One of the best sources of help is people who are already doing it, so tell your family and friends what you have in mind and listen to their experiences. See Chapter 3 for suggestions on approaching your boss about doing some or all of your work at home, and for business ideas if you would like to be self-employed.

8–10   You are almost at the point where you can move to working from home. Which statements are still not true for you? Are they factors you can change or are they dependent on someone else? Once you have checked the chapters mentioned above, take a look at Chapter 7 so that you don't become isolated and Chapter 8 for details on establishing boundaries for work and home.

Resources

☐ Your best friend – making such a fundamental change as working from home is always easier when you have support from someone who believes in you, so talk to them now about your plans.

☐ *Free Agent Nation: How America's New Independent Workers Are Transforming the Way We Live* by Daniel Pink. Warner Books, 2001.
Already regarded as a classic, Pink's book analyses the shift from twentieth century mass employment by large corporations to the 'free agents', including large numbers of homeworkers, who are changing the face of politics and the family as well as business.

☐ www.homeworking.com
An excellent source of information on all kinds of homeworking, including a forum where you can ask questions and share experiences.

☐ www.motheratwork.co.uk
A webzine for parents that includes articles, job vacancies and a directory of employers with a good record of supporting employees' work/life balance.

☐ www.careerathome.co.uk
If you are thinking about working from home, or need some information about a particular aspect of homeworking, this site has useful articles on a range of subjects, and a free monthly newsletter.

☐ www.workwiseuk.org
Work Wise UK is a not-for-profit initiative that encourages smarter working practices including working from home. Their website provides information on the benefits of home working and how they are promoting smarter working in the UK, including Work Wise Week and National Work from Home Day.

☐ www.tca.org.uk
The Telework Association is a membership organisation offering information to those who work flexibly. You pay for membership but nonmembers can read back issues of the electronic magazine for free on the Magazine page.

☐ www.liveworkhomes.co.uk
If you'd like to know more about the environmental benefits of homeworking, this readable site provides fascinating facts and figures to show how living and working in the same place can help to save time, money and the planet.

2
WILL WORKING FROM HOME WORK FOR ME?

Regardless of the type of job you do, working from home has its own unique demands, which you must be able to fulfil at the same time as carrying out your job effectively. Time and again, the people I spoke to while researching this book told me that they considered certain characteristics to be essential for working from home. The ones mentioned most often, and the ones that seem to cause the most concern to new homeworkers, are self-discipline and self-motivation. It's vital to be able to motivate yourself to get started on your work and continue until you've finished each task, even though nobody is keeping an eye on you and nobody may know how much you are achieving.

Of course, if you're used to working with other people, it's hard to know how self-disciplined and self-motivated you would be when working from home until you try it. The best way to start assessing your suitability for homeworking is by finding out about some key aspects of your personality. If you are already a homeworker, this information will help you to understand yourself better and recognise what is blocking you from becoming more successful.

This chapter provides some simple insights into your personality:

1. How different traits affect your performance as a homeworker.

2. How you perceive the world – whether you are a visual, auditory or kinaesthetic type, and how knowing your type can help you to learn, relate to people and express your appreciation.

4. What motivates you – are you a 'towards' person or an 'away' person?

5. Your attitude to time and schedules – are you in-time or through-time?

6. What prompts you to make a decision – are you proactive or reactive?

7. Assess how well you would respond to working from home by completing the questionnaire.

You will find out how your brain is wired, and whether it is presently wired in a way that is helpful for homeworking. If there is room for improvement, you will learn some strategies for coping more effectively.

This kind of self-awareness means that you are able to observe yourself objectively and acknowledge when you need to make changes. Self-discipline and self-motivation then allow you to make the changes in your behaviour which will get you better results. Working from home can be a crash course in getting to know yourself better if you are open-minded and willing to change.

A Designer's Story

Kevin fell into working from home as a designer without too much thought. 'My first reaction was "Oh, great, now I don't have to get up so early!" and I did stay in bed late for a while, but in the end I decided that I needed to be more disciplined, and so I started getting up earlier. Recently I realised I was spending a lot of my working time reading new product information. Keeping up to date is crucial in my industry, but sometimes it might not be the highest priority. And I'd also started wasting time by watching videos on the internet, which wasn't productive at all. So I decided to analyse my use of time more closely and I got hold of one of those timers you see at chess matches. Now I time how long I take on different tasks (see Chapter 5, page 83) because in a sense, when you work from home, time is more precious as you could be doing something else, like playing with the kids, and I want to be sure I'm not wasting time.'

Sometimes it's necessary not only to be aware of your own behaviour and to manage it so you produce better results when working from home, but also to manage your behaviour in relation to other people. I had many opportunities to learn the reality of this while running my cleaning business and juggling the needs of my cleaners and my clients, but there is one memory which stands out.

The Millionaire on the Doorstep

‘ *One of my office cleaners once asked for the evening off and I reluctantly had to stand in for her. As I was grumpily polishing the brass step at the office doorway, which was shared by the restaurant next door, a man in a suit passed me on his way to the restaurant, saying "When you've done that, you can come and do mine." The thoughts that ran through my mind were unprintable, but out of politeness and the knowledge I was representing my business, I replied with a remark I no longer recall, but was no doubt just as banal.*

To my surprise the man turned back, saying "I could do with somebody with a sense of humour to do my cleaning. All my cleaners are old and grumpy." I assumed he meant house cleaning and told him I didn't do that. "No, no," he replied, "I mean office cleaning."

"Oh," I said, "do you have an office round here?"

"Yes," he replied and told me his name – that of the richest man in the area, the self-made multi-millionaire founder of a greetings card company. He asked me for a business card and made an appointment there and then for me to visit one of his many properties and quote for the cleaning. I was offered the job, and over the next few months took on more and more work until he became my biggest client, as he still was when I sold the business several years later.

I've dined out on that story many times and always been grateful for that chance meeting on the brass doorstep, but it's only while thinking about this chapter that I've realised that I wouldn't have got the opportunity if I'd given in to my bad temper and replied rudely or not at all. Luckily I didn't take out my bad mood on a passing stranger and that fact brought me a huge amount of work.

Just a thought

The information in this chapter is provided to help you get to know yourself better, to improve your self-awareness and help you to succeed in working from home. There is no question of any of the descriptions in the rest of the chapter being 'right' or 'wrong' or one 'better' than another. They are simply starting points. Knowledge is power – once you are aware you operate in a certain way, you have the choice to make changes if you wish and if it suits your circumstances.

Why personality matters

Personality testing, also known as personality profiling, is widely used by employers and you may already have taken such a test as part of a recruitment or promotion procedure or on a training course. In business the most widely used personality profiles ask a series of questions about your behaviour preferences and use your answers to identify where you are on four indices. Three of these were created in the 1920s by Carl Jung, the German psychologist, in his study of people's psychological preferences and the way that these affect their way of dealing with life. The fourth was added later.

You can now find out more about your preferences (extrovert/introvert, sensing/intuition, thinking/feeling and judging/perceiving) by ticking which of the following statements you agree with. Although your answers may not fit neatly into one category or the other, you will gain an understanding of how each affects your performance as a homeworker, and in each section I provide suggestions as to how each type might improve their happiness and performance while working from home. If you tick the same number of questions for each type, it suggests you are able to balance this part of your personality and you should cope well with the aspects of homeworking related to it.

EXTROVERT AND INTROVERT

Jung coined the terms 'extroversion' and 'introversion', from the Latin words 'extra', meaning outside, 'intro', meaning inward and 'vertere' which means to turn. So an extrovert turns to the outside for inspiration, often to other people, and an introvert turns inside to their own resources. To find whether you tend towards introversion or extroversion, ask yourself these questions.

Do you

a) get changed after a hard day at work and head off to the pub for an evening chatting with friends?

b) tend to speak before fully thinking through what you want to say?

c) have many friends and acquaintances?

d) have a quiet night in with a good book or favourite television programme after a hard day at work?

e) often get told you are a good listener?

f) have just a few very close friends you can confide in?

If you answered yes to questions a) to c), you have extrovert tendencies. You get energy from other people and seek out company.

If you answered yes to d) to f), you have introvert tendencies.

The extrovert type

If you are the extrovert type, you like plenty of action and do not need much time for reflection. Your love of company may mean you find working alone boring and demoralising, so if working from home is to be successful and enjoyable, you will need to maintain a strong support network. The positive side is that at home you tend to have more freedom to do this than in a conventional office environment.

The introvert type

If you are the introvert type you get energy by looking within yourself and so you can find other people draining. You are interested in thoughts and ideas, and tend to be solitary and self-sufficient. Being happy with your own company will make working from home appealing, but you will still need contact with others. You may get the most out of networking by restricting the number and length of meetings you organise to allow yourself plenty of thinking time afterwards.

Coping with isolation

Bearing in mind that isolation is generally regarded as the number one challenge in working from home, it's easy to see how your degree of extroversion or introversion will have a big impact on how comfortable you feel working from home. Being an extrovert does not rule out the possibility of working from home, however. It is mainly a question of understanding your own needs and adapting your habits accordingly. In fact it's so important that I've devoted the whole of Chapter 7 to the subject of isolation and how to stay connected even if you are working alone.

And of course nobody is entirely extrovert or entirely introvert; we are all at different points on a sliding scale, and we can move up and down the scale depending on circumstances. An introvert may be the life and soul of the party with family or old friends they are comfortable with; an extrovert may dread the prospect of a function where they know no-one.

We can also train ourselves to cope with situations outside our comfort zone if there is sufficient motivation, for example, if your job description demands that you entertain clients. Sometimes people are so good at putting on a show that others are amazed when they confess it is really an effort and not a natural part of their personality at all.

A Magazine Owner's Story

Toni runs a business magazine from home with her husband Nick, who previously worked as a journalist for national publications. As they have complementary skills, they make a good team and it was obvious from the start how they would split responsibilities. Nick is happy with his own company and writes and edits the content of the magazine in their home office, an old farmhouse at the end of a long lane. Before having her children, Toni had a career selling magazine advertising space. She is chatty and interested in people.

So it is Toni who goes out every day to attend countless networking meetings and talk to prospective and current customers. I have seen her in action – her energy and enthusiasm are boundless and she talks openly and cheerfully to all kinds of people, from the catering staff to the most influential guest. Yet even Toni, a natural extrovert, says her networking style is partly a facade, only possible because she is so determined to establish their business and give their children a comfortable lifestyle. Nick confirms that she would never be this outgoing in a more informal situation.

SENSING AND INTUITION

Sensing and intuition are the terms Jung used to describe how individuals take in information and perceive the world. To find out whether you tend towards sensing or intuition, ask yourself the following questions.

Do you

a) describe yourself as down-to-earth and practical?

b) show more interest in detail than the big picture?

c) enjoy getting tangible results?

d) think of yourself as open to inspiration and hunches?

e) prefer the big picture to getting down to detail?

f) find routine work difficult to finish?

If you answered yes to questions a) to c), you are what Jung termed a sensing type.

If you answered yes to questions d) to f), you are intuitive.

Sensing types, as the term suggests, rely heavily on what their five senses are telling them and trust this information as it is their own direct experience. They are interested in what is happening right now, and they value order and systems. Intuitive types are more interested in what might be called their 'gut feelings' and the inspiration these feelings provide. They are fascinated by the future, are open to possibilities and are more likely to be innovators.

THE SENSING TYPE

If you are the sensing type you tend to adapt well to homeworking as you focus naturally on the day-to-day, practical aspects of getting your work done. You set up your own systems to make sure processes happen at the right time, and put checks in place to make doubly sure. You are good at planning and get satisfaction from knowing that everything is in place. But this emphasis on present efficiency can make you neglect strategic planning for the future and hesitant to take up opportunities when a leap of faith is needed.

THE INTUITIVE TYPE

If you are the intuitive type you excel at strategic thinking as you are a fast thinker whose mind jumps effortlessly from one subject to another. As you are more likely to be thinking about the future than the day-to-day systems required by homeworking, you get bored with routine work and tend to hop erratically from one task to another. As a homeworker, you might want to consider getting help with routine tasks like correspondence and record-keeping.

Sensing and Intuition in Practice

' *My partner is an intuitive type, while I am sensing. In the past this has caused problems when we have been discussing plans for our business. A pattern emerged where Andy would come up with what he considered to be a wonderful idea, and I would respond by immediately bringing up all the potential problems. He would be hurt by what he saw as my negativity, and I would wonder why he could ever imagine such a wild idea was remotely realistic. After many arguments we have finally learnt that we both want to achieve the same thing – a successful, vibrant business – but are coming at it from different directions.* '

THINKING AND FEELING

Thinking and feeling relate to the different types of information we use to make decisions. To find out how you go about making decisions, answer these questions:

Do you

a) base your decisions on objective information?

b) make a point because it is logical and not because it will keep the peace?

c) prefer to tell the truth even if people don't want to hear it?

d) base decisions on other people's feelings?

e) put yourself out to accommodate the wishes of others?

f) try to avoid conflict?

If you answered yes to questions a) to c), you are a thinking type.

If you answered yes to questions d) to f), you are a feeling type.

THE THINKING TYPE

If you are the thinking type you use objective information as the basis for your decisions. Getting a task completed is more important to you than relating to the people involved and how they might respond to you emotionally. When working from home, you need to remember to make time to keep in contact with people, just for its own sake. No matter how busy you are, the odd quick phone call or email just to check everything is OK will keep colleagues onside for when there's an emergency and you, the thinker, need their help.

THE FEELING TYPE

If you are the feeling type you make decisions based on subjective information – 'How do I feel about this?' – and on how decisions will affect others. You need to be disciplined when working from home in order not to spend too long on the phone, checking in with your colleagues. Try to keep your own goals in mind and don't be overly concerned with the opinions and feelings of others. Beware of the danger of being pulled into other people's problems. A confidant who understands your work will help you to keep things in perspective.

Who's the Thinker?

'Andy used to run our business on his own, but was struggling with the day-to-day admin and organisation. We decided that, as I have plenty of experience in this field, I should gradually take on more responsibility for looking after the finances, record-keeping, and so on. I may be more efficient in a rational, 'business-like' way, but often Andy doesn't like my suggestions because he feels they conflict with his personal values.

My business experience tells me he should ask his clients to sign a contract when they commit to using his training services, agreeing to pay on a sliding scale in the event of cancellation. Andy feels that this suggests he doesn't trust them, even though occasionally he has actually lost out financially through late cancellations. He wants to run things more on trust, while I want to get it all in black and white. Any idea what our preferences are?'

JUDGING AND PERCEIVING

Myers Briggs were a mother and daughter team of psychologists who in the 1940s added a fourth indicator to the three Jung had devised, and developed his theories into the method for understanding personality that is still widely used today. The judging and perceiving scale analyses how people respond to their environment. To find out which type you are, answer the following questions

Do you

a) like to plan and organise your life?

b) make decisions and abide by them?

c) pride yourself on your ability to stick at things?

d) like to be spontaneous and flexible?

e) prefer to keep your options open?

f) pride yourself on being open to change?

If you answered yes to questions a) to c), you are a judging type.

If you answered yes to questions d) to f), you are a perceiver.

To be a successful homeworker you must be able to balance your judging and perceiving tendencies. The perceiver can allow you to be spontaneous and take advantage of the freedom that working from home brings, whether it's in the form of unexpected good weather or a social visit, and the judge lets you enjoy the time off, knowing that you can trust yourself to catch up later.

THE PERCEIVING TYPE

If you are the perceiving type you may struggle with deadlines when working from home, as deadlines reduce your options and curtail your freedom. You may need to develop your own strategy to deal with this. A homeworker I know prides himself on delivering work as soon as he possibly can, regardless of how far-away the deadline is – that way he never really has to think about deadlines!

THE JUDGING TYPE

If you are the judging type who works from home you will have no problems with the self-discipline and organisation that others find so difficult to deal with. You have a carefully devised plan and you stick to it. Be careful not to miss out by failing to recognise opportunities if they don't conform to your plan, and don't let your ideas get too rigid or you'll lose some of your creativity.

A Businessman's Story

Pete sees himself as a natural entrepreneur. He has no trouble with coming up with new ideas, and often they are great ideas. But that in itself is a problem, as Pete is always convinced of the brilliance of the latest idea and is constantly trying to juggle lots of projects he doesn't have the time to see through to the end. He drives himself and his staff mad by splitting his attention between different tasks and abandoning the ones that don't seem to be working out as quickly as he'd hoped. A little more of the judging quality would give him a chance to establish an idea and develop his business.

Why people see things differently

The brain takes in information in five different ways and at any time we may be most aware of what we are seeing (visual sense), hearing (auditory sense), physically feeling (kinaesthetic sense), smelling (olfactory sense), or tasting (gustatory sense). The first three – visual, auditory and kinaesthetic – are the most important in the context of working from home:

☐ The visual sense allows you to see both what is happening around you – the people walking by – and the images you are creating in your own head.

☐ Your auditory sense enables you to hear the sounds of the outside world, like traffic passing, and what you are saying to yourself – we all hear voices in our heads!

☐ The kinaesthetic sense provides physical sensations like the rain against your face, and inner bodily feelings like hunger.

You experience the world through a combination of all the senses, but often you have a favourite, or predominant, sense. Knowing whether you are a visual, auditory or kinaesthetic type is useful to those who work from home, as it helps you to organise your workspace and understand the little quirks about how you work.

You can find out which senses you and other people favour by listening closely to the language you habitually use. For example, if you say 'I see what you mean', you are currently using your visual system. 'I hear what you're saying' means the auditory system predominates. 'I'm feeling out of touch' suggests the kinaesthetic system is uppermost. You may have a favourite system, closely followed by another. It wasn't until it was pointed it out to me that I realised how often I say 'I'll see how I feel' (visual, kinaesthetic) when somebody proposes a plan.

I have a strong visual sense and get very irritable when my desk and office are messy. It sounds horribly obsessive, but I just can't get started on any work until I have tidied up and got myself organised. Those who favour the auditory sense may hate working in a noisy environment or in a place where they could be disturbed. People who are more kinaesthetic may have strong opinions about the kind of desk and chair they use and need to be comfortably settled before they can concentrate. All of these factors are important considerations when you are organising your workspace at home.

UNDERSTANDING HOW YOU LEARN

Our dominant sense also has a major bearing on how we learn. As homeworkers, knowing how we learn most quickly and easily is very helpful as generally we have to take responsibility ourselves for assimilating new information, often in a limited period of time.

Learning for the visual type

You will learn best by being able to look at instructions or an illustration, so e-learning programmes will suit you. I can assimilate information much more easily if I can read it or look at it for myself. I hate people reading articles to me out of the paper, as it slows down my process of understanding.

Learning for the auditory type

You will learn best by listening to a lecture or to instructions given verbally, so e-learning with a strong auditory element may be useful. Tapes and CDs will suit you and are especially handy if you are short of time, as you can listen in the car. Even when not consciously listening, you will take in a huge amount of information.

Learning for the kinaesthetic type

You will want to handle equipment or actually carry out a process yourself in order to learn a new skill. Have you ever tried learning a new procedure on the computer by watching someone else do it? I might be visual, but my kinaesthetic sense is close behind, and I find watching someone else explain a program, whether in a lecture or a one-to-one situation, infuriating and impossible to absorb. My hand itches to get hold of the mouse and move it to the relevant places myself.

So if you are having difficulty learning something, don't beat yourself up by worrying about being dense, try to get hold of the information in a format which strongly relates to your preferred type(s). If the material is put across differently, you are likely to pick it up much more easily.

UNDERSTANDING HOW YOU RELATE TO PEOPLE

When you work from home you are often working independently without an intermediary, so it is important for you to establish and maintain good working relationships and not rely on PAs or colleagues to do it for you. If you listen carefully to your colleagues and clients, you will get a sense of their preferred type. (Although bear in mind that we all use all the senses, and the predominant type we use may change according to our mood and the situation we are in.)

If you use words and phrases which fit their preferred sense (see the Just a thought box above for examples), you are less likely to come away from a conversation with someone with the feeling that although you had both understood each individual word spoken, no real communication had actually occurred. You will stop trying to make them 'see' something they just weren't 'hearing'! You might also find that you develop much stronger relationships with the people you meet through work, whether they are clients, suppliers or employees.

UNDERSTANDING HOW TO SAY THANK YOU

We tend to treat people in the way we would like to be treated ourselves, but this doesn't always have the desired effect, and then we are puzzled and perhaps feel hurt and rejected. The detailed knowledge and understanding you develop by working closely with people as a homeworker can be put to good use.

Thanking visual types

Your colleague with a visual preference will like to see how grateful you are for their contribution. They will enjoy receiving a thank you card or a bunch of flowers they can display. Remember that appearance is very important to them, so make sure you are always dressed appropriately whenever you meet them.

Thanking auditory types

Others may need to hear how well they are doing, and not just in the kind of words spoken, but also in the tone of voice that is used. They may be very sensitive to offhand or sarcastic comments.

Thanking kinaesthetic types

If your colleague is a kinaesthetic type, they may be more likely than others to express physical affection in a work situation, so don't be surprised to get a hug when you were expecting a handshake!

Just a thought
Once you know what makes you tick, you won't get so wound up.

What makes you get up in the morning?

Self-motivation is one of the biggest fears people have about working from home. 'How do I know I won't spend the whole day watching television in my dressing gown?' is a common question. I think most people find the need to pay the mortgage and satisfy their boss or customers fairly pressing, but it's a good question.

This section will help you to understand what motivates you on a fundamental level, not just the pressure of paying the bills and with luck having some spending money left over. Once you understand this, the issue of getting work done while working on your own at home should be less of a worry. It will also help you to understand why some people do things differently from you, which might mean you can avoid conflict in the future over these different habits. Read the questions below and think about which kind of person you generally tend to be, bearing in mind we are all complex characters and do not fit neatly into boxes. You might like to write your answers down so you can analyse them thoroughly.

WHAT MOTIVATES YOU?

Let's use working from home as an example. Have a think about why you already work from home, or the reasons you are thinking about doing so. What do you want to achieve and what is important to you?

For example, do you want to get away from the drudge of the daily commute? Maybe you can do without the politics and interruptions at work. Perhaps you resent spending so much of your hard-earned salary on travel.

Do you think you can have a better quality of life working at home? Or do you want to have more time with your partner or children? Maybe you believe you can live a more healthy lifestyle if you can prepare all your own meals.

When you've written down your own reasons for working from home, have another look at the first paragraph of suggested reasons above. This is a list of things you dislike and want to get 'away from'. The second paragraph lists the things you like and want to move 'toward'. Look at what you've written down. Are they things you want to move away from, things you don't want? Or are they things you do want, the things you want to move toward? If you're not sure which predominate in this context, try thinking about other aspects of your life, like your choice of house, holiday and friends. Do you tend to make choices to get away from what you don't like, or to move toward the things you do? Just knowing which approach you naturally opt for helps you to choose goals which inspire you.

MOTIVATED AWAY FROM

If we think in terms of the old 'carrot and stick' scenario, the generally 'away from' person responds better to being given something they dislike and want to move away from – the stick in other words. They will be motivated by the need to perform well enough not to be fired or to avoid situations and tasks they don't enjoy.

MOTIVATED TOWARD

The generally 'toward' person responds better to the 'carrot' so promises of a pay rise or promotion will be more motivating to them. A threat of something unpleasant will not motivate a 'toward' person, just make them very cross.

Motivating yourself

❝ *I tend to be an "away from" person and I find that I can get hooked back into the negative emotion of the situation or thing I want to get away from, and getting unstuck can be hard work. By consciously applying the 'toward' strategy, it's easier to be pulled forward by the excitement and attraction of the goal I'm aiming for. Try it for yourself and see what works best.* ❞

Look out for this in other people's conversation too and it will come in handy when you need to get something done. When it's the 'carrot or stick' scenario, the skill is in knowing whether it's appropriate to dangle the carrot or apply the stick!

How do you keep time?

Understanding how you think about time is a helpful predictor of how well you are likely to be able to manage your time when you work from home and there is no-one to clock-watch for you. What kind of person are you where dealing with time is concerned?

ARE YOU ALWAYS ON TIME – OR ALWAYS LATE?

Do you often check the clock and usually know roughly what time it is? Do you like to be punctual? Even though you may be concentrating on one task, are you still aware of time passing and of the next appointment in your diary?

Or maybe you tend to get so absorbed in what you're doing that you lose track of time. You might tell your colleague you are about to do something and then get distracted by another job, and then something else, and forget what you were doing in the first place.

You probably recognise these different attitudes to time and maybe they drive you crazy. The first person is 'through-time' and the second is 'in-time'. 'Through-time' people are always punctual and get annoyed waiting for their 'in-time' friend who is invariably late and arrives breathless with tales of all the things they got caught up by.

THROUGH-TIME PEOPLE

Through-time people who work from home are likely to have less trouble with time management. As you have a sense of time passing, you will be able to plan chunks of time to complete specific tasks, while remembering what is happening next. If you are meeting someone who is in-time, you could try getting there a bit later than arranged, or take along something to read so you aren't wasting time until they turn up.

IN-TIME PEOPLE

In-time people need some time management strategies when working from home. You might set your mobile or alarm clock to remind you to move on to another job. You tend to get bored with a task quicker than through-time people, so try to spend another ten minutes on your work after you have started to feel fed up and you'll get lots more done. If you find it difficult to prioritise your work, write down all the jobs you have to do in strict order of priority (there is more on this in Chapter 5, page 88) and stick to it, only moving on when you have completed each one.

It Drives Me Mad

❝ It is funny how often couples seem to have opposite qualities – I am through-time and Andy is in-time. As we both work at home we often decide to have a break at a certain time to go out for a walk or have a coffee, but I find I need to remind him about fifteen minutes before, or time will drift by until it is too late to bother. Sometimes he tells me he is about to start supper and then almost an hour later, when I'm starving and go in search of food, I find he hasn't moved from the computer! Now that I know about through-time and in-time, I understand it a bit more, but it can still be infuriating. ❞

Decisions, decisions

When working from home, there is nobody else to tell you what to do and how to react when a decision needs to be made. This section will help you to understand whether you find it easy to take decisions or not, and what kind of work is best suited to you as a homeworker. Which description below best sums up your attitude to decision-making?

1. Do you wait until you simply have to respond to an issue? Would you rather let other people decide what should happen?

2. Or do you like to take things into your own hands, act now and think later? Does bureaucracy enrage you?

REACTIVE AND PROACTIVE

If the first description sums you up, you are what is known as a 'reactive' person. The second description describes a 'proactive' person who is good at getting things done. The type of work you do may indicate which type you are – proactive types make good salespeople, reactive types are good at analysing and researching. Think about people you know and the jobs they do. Can you classify them accordingly?

Just because you tend to be reactive does not mean you shouldn't work from home, as there are plenty of jobs where your work flow is controlled by your manager or outside factors or where you are required to respond to an external demand, such as telephone enquiries coming in to your phone line at home. But if you are thinking of becoming self-employed, you should realise that it will demand a higher level of being, or learning to be, proactive. You may already be proactive in some situations and reactive in others – often we behave differently at home to the way we do at work, for example – and just need to get used to applying that strength in a different context.

QUESTIONNAIRE – ARE YOU SUITED TO HOMEWORKING?

All of the people I talked to when researching this book believed that certain personality traits are vital if you are to be able to work happily and efficiently from home.

This questionnaire helps you to assess how well you might adapt to working from home. Consider each statement below in terms of whether it is generally true or false for you. Don't think about it too hard or answer as you wish you were – just go with what feels right. Give yourself one point for each statement you feel is true and then check your score. This questionnaire is just an indication of how easily you may adapt to working from home, so always trust your own instincts – it's a good habit to get into.

☐ I am confident in assessing the quality of my work and making changes when necessary.

☐ I am happy to speak to anybody on the phone, regardless of their job title.

☐ I can set my own goals and plan a schedule to achieve them, without consulting others.

☐ I work best when I am not disturbed by interruptions.

☐ I can bounce back from rejection and setbacks without telling my friends first.

☐ I am resourceful in a crisis.

☐ I can switch off when the working day is over and enjoy my free time.

☐ I am flexible and can change my plans at short notice.

☐ I have a supportive framework of friends and colleagues, both inside and outside work.

☐ I can motivate myself to embark on a project and follow it through.

☐ I like making decisions.

☐ I am happy in my own company.

☐ I can cope with deadlines and have worked out my own strategy for dealing with them.

☐ I am able to define boundaries for my family and friends and ensure my working time is not unnecessarily disturbed.

☐ I can stay focused in the face of distractions.

☐ I can organise information, both online and paper, and then find it quickly when needed.

Your score:

0–4   It seems that you may struggle with the realities of working from home, perhaps because your natural inclination would be to spend your time with other people who can act as a sounding board, or perhaps because you have never thought of yourself in these terms before. Take stock and discuss it with someone you can trust to be honest before making any decisions. Chapter 1 will help to clarify your reasons for wanting to work from home and Chapter 2 will help to examine your personality and how it will have an impact on your performance.

5–8   You may want to spend some time developing skills relating to self-reliance and motivation before starting to work from home. All of these abilities can be learned and you may just need some practice. Ask your boss at work to start encouraging you to work on your own more, and find out whether that feels like something you would want to do more of. Take a look at Chapter 3 for some ideas on making money at home, and Chapter 5 to give you a hand with working more productively.

9–12   You already have some of the characteristics required for working from home. If you can work on the aspects you are less strong at, you should have a very good chance of making a success of it as well as enjoying yourself. Be sure to keep in regular touch with other people so that you do not feel isolated. Chapter 7 will help you to establish strong networks to help you stay connected and motivated. Read Chapter 6 if you are wondering how to maintain a professional image when working from the kitchen table.

13–16   You are obviously very self-motivated and have many of the qualities needed to work successfully from home. You should find that you adapt well and soon find your feet. You may need to be careful that you don't fall into the classic homeworking trap of forgetting how to switch off and thinking about work 24 hours a day. If you are concerned about blurring work and home life, read Chapter 8 on establishing boundaries. Chapter 9 will reassure you that you can cope if it all goes pear-shaped.

Resources

☐ Your mother or someone who knows you very well – if you're not sure what kind of person you are in any of the categories in this chapter, they will certainly know.

☐ *Emotional Intelligence* by Daniel Goleman. Bloomsbury, 1996.
Daniel Goleman's first, groundbreaking book about why understanding your emotions and how to manage them can be more important than your IQ level to achieving success.

☐ *Working with Emotional Intelligence* by Daniel Goleman. Bloomsbury, 1999.
A sequel applying Emotional Intelligence to the world of work. It gives lots of corporate anecdotes but is of equal use to interested homeworkers.

☐ *Principles of NLP* by J. O'Connor and I. McDermott. Thorsons, 1996.
Now out of print but available secondhand on Amazon, this is a concise and readable introduction to Neuro-Linguistic Programming, the rather sinister name for the study of how our upbringing and experience have programmed our own brains with the language we use, the effect this has on our behaviour and how we can re-program ourselves to get better results. The sections in this chapter on self-motivation, dealing with time and decision-making are my own, simplified interpretations of NLP.

☐ www.andrewbibby.com/telework/why_twk.html
An extract from writer and journalist Andrew Bibby's 1991 book *Home is Where the Office is*, now out of print. This chapter will help you to assess if homeworking is right for you.

☐ www.andybritnell.co.uk
The website for our training and coaching company where you can read more about personality profiling as an aid to self-awareness and purchase your own detailed profile, followed by a coaching session on how to adapt your personal qualities to homeworking.

3

CAN I MAKE MONEY AT HOME?

Over the last century or so it has become so normal to go out to work, in a location away from the home, that you might be wondering whether it is actually possible to stay at home and still earn a living. The answer to that question in many cases is 'yes', and if it's not currently, then with a little planning and application, it could be at some point in the not-too-distant future.

This chapter covers:

1. A warning about heavily advertised homeworking 'opportunities'.

2. Factors to think about if you are employed and would like to work from home.

3. How to negotiate with your boss to work from home.

4. Different ways of making a self-employed income at home.

5. Dealing with the red tape of self-employment.

6. Some basic points about managing money when you work for yourself.

7. Who to ask for help when you are self-employed.

Homeworking 'opportunities' – approach with caution

Making a little extra money at home, either after work or between household and family commitments, is an attractive possibility for many people. That means there is a large market for the type of con artist who plays on people's insecurity in order to make a quick buck. You've probably seen adverts stuck on lampposts at busy traffic junctions, displayed in the back of a car or inserted in the jobs section of the local paper – something along the lines of 'Earn £1000 a day working part time from home'.

Or you might have received unsolicited emails or seen the adverts on search engine sites offering high earnings 'with cast-iron guarantee' for operating an online business. These adverts are carefully worded to appeal to people a bit short of money who could do with making some cash fast. They play on the human desire to believe in something that sounds like a quick and easy answer to a problem, while not looking too hard at the facts. Does it sound too good to be true? Then unfortunately it *is* too good to be true.

If an advert seems plausible, but on enquiring further, you are asked to send money up-front, either as a registration fee or to buy stock, the alarm bells should start ringing. Have you ever been asked to pay anything when applying for a job? I doubt it. If a payment is requested, someone is trying to rip you off.

For more information on how to spot a homeworking scam and to read about experiences other people have had, visit www.homeworking.com. The site includes a forum where you can post your own experiences and ask fellow users for their feedback.

Is working from home as an employee the right step?

There are many factors to consider before deciding to work from home, relating to your own ambitions and your circumstances as well as your employers'. Don't assume that working from home is impossible for you, just because you are working for someone else. Your boss may simply have not thought of the idea themselves yet and might be open to the prospect if you introduce it in the right way. Here are some things to think about as you weigh up the idea.

IS WORKING FROM HOME THE RIGHT OPTION FOR MY CAREER AND PERSONAL ASPIRATIONS?

As we saw in Chapter 1, one of the downsides of working from home is that you inevitably lose some of your visibility with colleagues and bosses. If you are ambitious and want promotion, you need to consider whether or not your chances will be adversely affected by working from home. Chapter 6 covers ways of staying in touch with your colleagues and bosses, but will these be sufficient to give you the exposure you need to develop your career?

A Marketing Manager's Story

Rachel is the mother of a four-year-old and works from home for the majority of the time but makes a long monthly journey for team meetings. 'When I go to meetings,' she says, 'I find that higher management always remark "Oh, so you're Rachel. I've spoken to you but we've never met." It's clear that they know my name but not my face. That could be a problem but I've made the decision to work from home for the lifestyle, and for my daughter, not for my career.'

IS WORKING FROM HOME RIGHT FOR MY FAMILY AND HOME ENVIRONMENT?

Unless you live alone in glorious isolation, you will need to consider the impact of homeworking on your home life and family. If you are house-sharing with people who have different working patterns or who don't work, you may struggle to find the time and space to concentrate on work. How will working from home fit in with looking after children or elderly relatives? What will happen in the school holidays? It's vital your family understand how the change will affect them, and their role in making it run smoothly, before you start working from home. Chapter 8 looks at ways to achieve this with your partner and children.

CAN I ASK MY EMPLOYER TO LET ME WORK FROM HOME?

Any employee can *ask* their employer for flexible working arrangements, which can include job sharing, varying working hours, taking holidays at specific times of year or, the interesting bit as far as we are concerned, working from home for part or all of the week. However, the parents of children under six years old and disabled children under 18 years old, and the carers of some adults, have the *right* to apply to their employers to work flexibly and employers have the statutory duty to seriously consider such requests (note that the duty is only to consider, not necessarily to grant). The government has also announced plans to extend this right to all employees with children under 16 years old.

The employee must demonstrate that the requested flexible working arrangements are viable and will not have a negative impact on the business. The employer must consider the request and may reject it if it will, for example, entail extra costs or have a negative impact on business performance or the organisation of work among other staff.

The website of the Department of Business Enterprise and Regulatory Reform (DBERR), supplied in the Resources section at the end of this chapter, gives comprehensive information on your rights, the employer's duty and the procedure to follow, including templates for an application for flexible working. But in order to stand the best chance of success with your application to work from home, first have a good look at your particular circumstances to decide if working from home is a realistic option for you.

IS MY COMPANY LIKELY TO ALLOW ME TO WORK FROM HOME?

As we've seen, although you may request flexible working, your employer can still refuse your request if they believe there are good business reasons to do so.

Having spoken to a number of homeworkers about how they managed to negotiate homeworking with their bosses, it seems that there are two important factors at play here. One is the culture of the organisation and its openness to change, and the other is you and your relationship with your boss and colleagues.

Company culture

If you work for a business with an old-fashioned outlook – and by that I mean a very structured organisation with a clear hierarchy and its own bureaucratic way of doing things – it will probably be more difficult to convince them of the benefits of homeworking than a more forward-thinking business. A traditional company may still think in terms of staff being physically present in the office rather than what they produce and whether this can be achieved elsewhere. Particularly if you are the first person to ask to work from home, there may well be concerns about the quantity, quality and delivery of the work you will be producing.

A Sales Executive's Story

Sarah found out how resistant employers can still be to the idea of homeworking when she moved to a rural area from the Home Counties: 'At first I worked for a local employer but my salary was low, and I thought my prospects would be better with a company based outside the area that would pay me London rates to use my sales skills at home. Over the course of a year I kept applying for jobs but they couldn't get their heads around the idea of not having someone in the office. Finally I responded to an advert placed for an office-based person, and managed to convince the company to give me a chance of doing the job at home – but only after a three hour interview!'

Seven years later she is still in the same post, the main breadwinner of the family, earning more than double her previous salary – from home. Interestingly, many more people in the company now work from home too, since Sarah has proved that it is possible to get good results without being in the office.

Some companies have taken up homeworking with alacrity, seeing all the benefits of cost-cutting and improved productivity and morale mentioned in Chapter 1. BT is an acknowledged leader, having started out with 400 teleworkers ten years ago. 12000 people now work at home for BT and 63,000 are on some kind of flexible working arrangement. If homeworking is your ultimate goal, it will pay to do some research and make enquiries about prospective employers' attitudes to homeworking whenever you apply for a job.

Your reputation at work

This is really the crux of the matter. No matter how enlightened and progressive your employers, there is no way they will entertain the idea of you working from home if you are known for slapdash work, poor timekeeping or difficulty in relating to customers and colleagues. They will want to keep you right where they can see you. It's up to you to be brutally honest with yourself on this one. If there have been problems in the past, sort them out and make sure you're on an even keel before broaching the idea of working from home.

On the other hand, if you are a valuable employee, your bosses may be surprisingly flexible in order to retain you.

A Market Researcher's Story

After five years of living and working in central London, Sue was ready for a change of lifestyle, so she gave in her notice in order to move back to the area where she grew up. To her surprise her bosses responded by offering her the option of moving out of the central office, something she'd never even considered, because her contribution to current projects was so vital. After working for a while in a satellite office, she was able to negotiate full-time homeworking and has never been happier.

CAN I EASILY DO MY WORK AT HOME?

That should be a pretty straightforward one to answer. If you have responsibilities that tie you to the office, you might consider swapping these with a colleague to gain the freedom to work from home.

How to negotiate with your boss to work from home

You might want to use the DBERR template to make your application to work from home, but at some point you will need to sit down and talk to your boss. Give yourself the best chance of success by following these guidelines.

- ☐ You'll perhaps feel a little nervous about this conversation, especially if you have a lot invested in the prospect of working from home. Although you may feel that much is riding on this encounter, try to be relaxed and approach it from the perspective that a successful arrangement will benefit you *both* enormously. Explain clearly why you are making the request and the positive effect it will have on your work performance.

- ☐ Follow up with ideas as to how the arrangement could practically be put into operation, to show your boss that you have thought this through and are able to see things from their perspective as well. It will help if you have anticipated the objections that might be raised and can offer suggestions to overcome them.

- ☐ Give positive examples of other people you know who have made similar successful transitions, fitting them as closely to your own situation as possible.

An Exhibition Organiser's Story

Nicki had only been working for a small business for a few months when she and her family decided to move to a new area. Fortunately she had already established a good relationship with her boss: 'I told him that my sister-in-law lives in Antigua, and her work partner is in Barbados, so if they can make it work, I don't see why we can't!' And they do.

☐ Think in advance whether there are any cost-saving implications in your suggestion. Your company could save money on office space, heating and lighting costs etc. if fewer people are physically present.

☐ Give examples that show you are willing to be flexible in the new arrangements.

A Marketing Manager's Story

Rachel, the marketing manager mentioned previously, emphasises the importance of 'give-and-take' to the success of working from home and says she finds it very motivating to be trusted in this way. Due to her remote location, she has occasionally been stuck for a while without use of her computer: 'If there is an IT problem, as I only work four days a week, I take that day without computer access as my day off, regardless of any previous arrangements.'

☐ Suggest a trial period to test out the idea and see how it works in practice. Or try it out on a part-time basis, on the understanding that it will become full time if it works.

☐ Agree how to assess the effectiveness of your plan – will it be quantity or quality of output, maintaining good communication with other staff or a measure unique to your particular job? An objective yardstick will avoid the arrangement being jeopardised by someone who is prejudiced against homeworking or is envious of you.

☐ If you are not following the formal procedure outlined by DBERR (and there may be cases where it's better to adopt a more informal approach) it's advisable to put your agreement in writing, so that both parties understand exactly what has been agreed, for how long and how the results will be judged.

Tim, the magazine-editor-turned-consultant featured in Chapter 1, says that once he was working from home and organising his own time and workload, he *felt* like a freelancer, and from there it was an easy step to decide to make the move into self-employment. If you feel the time is right to start working for yourself, the next section is for you.

Making money at home as your own boss

It's estimated that about two thirds of homeworkers are people running their own businesses. Starting your own business at home is an attractive option if you are a parent wanting to fit work commitments around family, or if you are an employee who is under threat of redundancy or tired of corporate life. Setting up at home keeps your costs down while you test the market and find out if there is a demand for your product or service, and if you are suited to being your own boss.

> **It's a fact that...**
>
> more than half of all new businesses are run from home and more than 1400 new home businesses are started each week in the UK. Young people under 25 years old, mothers and those aged over 50 are particularly likely to start home businesses.
>
> Source: Enterprise Nation Home Business Report, 2007

Being self-employed and running a small business often turn out to be very different experiences than you imagined them to be. They demand qualities you may not have needed when you were working for someone else, such as the confidence and ability to go out and sell, the self-reliance to make your own decisions, and the resilience to keep going when times get difficult. Chapter 2 covers elements of self-awareness that may be useful if you haven't read it yet.

A Clinical Psychologist's Story

Susan used to work in an NHS hospital but left her job a year ago to start her own private practice: 'In some ways starting my own business and working from home have been more difficult than I anticipated. It has been challenging in so many different ways. I feel I've grown up a lot in the last year. I've really had to take personal responsibility; there's nobody else looking after me and I can't blame anybody else if things aren't going right. It's been good for me. Empowering is the word I'm looking for.'

WHAT KIND OF BUSINESS COULD YOU START?

There are a number of ways of becoming self-employed and they don't all involve having a brilliant and ground-breaking new business idea. We'll look at each option in turn and you'll find sources of more information in Resources at the end of the chapter.

Using your existing expertise

If you already have a skill or some expertise you are using as an employee, you can use the same skill on a self-employed basis. Many times I have heard people say that they are sick of making money for their employer and so they have decided to go it alone. This is great in principle, but you'll need to look carefully at the financial implications of your decision before making the leap, or you could find yourself worse off and possibly working harder than ever. We look at the financial implications of going freelance later in this chapter.

Buying a franchise

When you buy a franchise, you buy the permission to operate a business that has already proved successful elsewhere, so franchising is often considered a safer way to go into business than starting from scratch. Many high street names operate as franchises, including Clarks shoe shops, Kall-Kwik printers and Toni and Guy hairdressers. The cost of the franchise may include items such as operating manuals, stock, processes, systems and stationery. All this does, however, come at a price and you will lose your investment if the business fails. So it pays to do extensive research into your chosen franchise before committing yourself, and to remember at all times that the less scrupulous are more interested in getting their hands on your fee than in helping you succeed.

Buying an existing business

Taking over a business that has been up and running for a while might seem like a tempting prospect, but you need to do thorough research and negotiate the purchase price carefully to avoid being sold a white elephant. Decide before you start looking what kind of business you want and how much you can afford to pay.

Businesses for sale are listed in the national press, on the internet and in print publications like *Daltons Weekly*. You might find a business that is not being advertised by speaking to your professional advisers, who will know what's happening in the business world locally.

The Power of Word of Mouth

I sold my cleaning business after months of unsuccessful advertising when my accountants put out an email to their contacts to the effect that they knew of a small cleaning business for sale. Another accountant replied who just happened to be looking for a business for his mother-in-law, but he could equally well have been keeping an eye open for a client.

The key question is to find out why the business is being sold and it may not be easy to get a direct answer to this, unless the owner is ready to retire. The owner could come up with any number of reasons when the truth is that the business is not profitable.

So you need to carry out a process known as 'due diligence' where you examine the whole business. An accountant can help you to analyse the figures, but you should also look carefully at factors such as processes, key members of staff, competitors and trends in the market. A business is only worth the amount someone is willing to pay for it, so use the results of your due diligence to negotiate the price.

Direct selling, network marketing, multi level marketing (MLM), party plan

Direct selling means that the manufacturer sells direct to the customer with no retail middle man. As direct selling can easily be done from home on a part-time basis, it is an obvious choice for mothers and for employees wanting to start a small business while keeping on the day job. Sales can be made door to door by dropping off a catalogue and returning later to collect orders, as you will know if you have ever had an Avon or Kleeneze brochure pushed through your door. Or salespeople may sell by personal referral and talk to their family, friends, neighbours and other contacts in the hope of making a sale. They may also use party plan, in which they take the products along to gatherings of friends for demonstration and sampling, after which orders are taken.

You may have heard of network marketing, sometimes called multi-level marketing (MLM). This means that salesperson A recruits or sponsors person B to become a salesperson, and then gets a bonus related to the number of sales that B makes, as well the sales that B's own network or 'downline' make. Those who are successful at recruiting new salespeople can end up making a great deal of money, and these affluent lifestyles are used by network marketing companies to promote their recruitment activities. Pictures of big houses and shiny cars are appealing to us all, so how do you make an informed decision about which company to join? Anne, who joined a network marketing company 18 months ago as a way of generating a retirement income, and has since astonished herself with her business and personal development, helped me to formulate some guidelines. (I am looking at this in detail as, unlike buying a franchise or business, which requires considerable research, a large outlay of capital and the advice of professionals, it is much easier and cheaper to start out in network marketing and you may find it harder to get objective advice.)

What to look for in a network marketing company

☐ Look for a company that is already well established. You need to know that it's going to be around in the future to provide the income you are working hard to generate now.

☐ Make sure the company trades ethically. Read the literature, go to the presentations and get a flavour of how business is done and how people behave towards you and each other.

☐ Find a company with a growing market. Think about what the company is selling and find out their market share. Is this something people are interested in buying more of or is it an industry going out of fashion or into decline?

☐ Be very selective about the products. They must be good quality and good value and you must be enthusiastic about using them yourself or you'll never sell them to other people.

☐ Consumables are the best option, something that is regularly used up and then reordered, as that way you can keep building your list of customers. If the products are one-off purchases you will constantly have to find new customers.

☐ There's another reason why it's important the products give good value – you've probably heard of pyramid selling and know that it's illegal. In pyramid selling there is little in the way of product and most of the money is made through recruitment, so that only the people in at the start of the scheme tend to benefit.

☐ How much support is available to me as a new salesperson? Reputable network marketing companies have developed sophisticated training systems to help you become effective quickly.

☐ It helps if your sponsor is local and you can meet up for support or to shadow them on meetings and presentations.

☐ Check that the company is a member of the Direct Selling Association which has strict codes of ethics its members must abide by.

Having spoken to a number of people who have been involved in network marketing, both successfully and unsuccessfully, I also have a few suggestions for things to bear in mind before making a decision.

Points to consider before joining a network marketing company

☐ Network marketing is not a get-rich-quick scheme, although it is possible to start making small amounts of money quickly.

☐ People who already run a business start network marketing with an advantage. Not only do they have an existing client base who might be interested in the products, but they have business and selling experience too.

☐ Those who have made a lot of money have worked hard for it and put in the time and commitment. Be clear about how much time and commitment you are willing to give.

☐ You should be equally clear about your goals. There are many reasons why people get involved – to earn a part-time income, to get out and meet people, to have an income in retirement etc. – and your sponsor won't be able to help you achieve your goals unless you both know what they are.

☐ To be successful you do not need to be a slick 'salesman' but you must enjoy talking to people. Joining a network marketing company will not change your basic personality traits or turn an introvert into an extrovert. If you have not already read Chapter 2, on how different personality types respond to working from home, you might like to look at it now.

☐ To be successful, you will have to push beyond your normal 'comfort zone' and do things that initially feel uncomfortable. But if you practise, those things will become normal and you will be able to push your comfort zone out further. Many people overlook this personal growth aspect when they get involved in network marketing.

☐ You may have a sponsor but you will also have to motivate yourself to learn and carry out all the jobs you need to do. You should be aware right from the start that there will be many ups and downs along the way.

INTERNET BUSINESSES

With stories regularly cropping up in the press about a geek with an internet idea making a million overnight, this can seem a tempting prospect for the homeworker. The word 'geek' here is a clue – unless you are passionate about IT and possess the appropriate skills, it's going to be a struggle, and paying someone else to do the technical stuff can get very expensive. If you have a brilliant idea, teaming up with an IT specialist can be an option, but bear in mind the points about partnerships made below.

Similarly if you're selling goods or services and hoping to expand your customer base, a website can seem like the ideal solution. But just adding yours to the millions already out there in cyberspace will achieve nothing unless prospective customers can find you in the first place, and then be sufficiently impressed by the quality of your offering to actually buy it. The search engine optimisation to achieve the former, and the design and programming to do the latter are both skills that are time consuming to learn and expensive to buy. Successful websites take time and effort to establish, and should not be regarded as a quick way to make money.

COMING UP WITH A BUSINESS IDEA

Many successful businesses are started by people who are looking for a specific product or service, feeling frustrated that nobody seems to provide it and deciding to do it themselves. Chrissie Rucker of The White Company did this in 1994 after failing to find good quality, affordable white bedlinen and towels in the high street. She started out in a room in her boyfriend's house where she packed the orders from her twelve-page mail order brochure until forced to find more space elsewhere. The White Company now has almost 20 shops in the UK and abroad, and an annual turnover of more than £50 million.

Sometimes you might take an existing business idea and twist it slightly, by improving the product you sell or upgrading its image.

A Step up the Ladder

In the 1980s my then husband was working for an estate agent in Bath and looking for a way to become self-employed. Talking to the owners of large houses outside the city, he spotted a gap in the market for a window cleaner with a smart image and good reputation, light years away from the stereotypical image of a bloke driving a rusty car with a couple of ladders on top. He bought a new Suzuki jeep, a fashionable vehicle in those days, had it smartly signwritten and used his estate agency contacts to get his first clients, who bought into his reputation and appearance.

Be open to the possibility that your original idea might transmute into something you would never have imagined at the outset. It's easy to fall in love with your idea and want to pursue it to the letter, but don't dismiss a deviation from your plan. If you look carefully at the long-term prospects of a new opportunity, you might find it actually offers more mileage.

Branching Out

After just a couple of months of window cleaning, my husband was offered an office cleaning contract by one of his window cleaning clients. We were surprised by the offer and at first doubtful, but on consideration we felt it might be a fruitful avenue to go down and accepted the contract. It was swiftly followed by other similar offers of work and just six months later I gave up my job to join the business and we took on our first employee. There is no way our business would have developed in the way it subsequently did if we had stuck with the window cleaning.

Getting to grips with the red tape of self-employment

This is the bit that self-employed people always complain about – unpalatable as it may be, as well as carrying out your business, satisfying your customers and doing your bookwork efficiently, you must now also act as an unpaid administrator for the government. I have never met anyone starting a new business who is not taken aback by the amount of official paperwork it involves.

Ignorance is no defence when it comes to business bureaucracy and you are expected to find out what your legal obligations are and to fulfil them on time, regardless of what else is happening in your business. If you do not, there may be financial and legal penalties.

Fortunately there is plenty of help available from all government departments and business advice organisations. But you do need to ask. Listed below are the legalities you should be aware of, and there is information on where to get more help on all of these issues in the Resources section at the end of this chapter. You should also check in case there are other legal issues specific to your industry relating to qualifications, licences, ongoing training, and so on.

CHOOSING THE STATUS OF YOUR BUSINESS

You need to decide the legal status of your business before you set up, as at the most basic level it affects the type and amount of tax and National Insurance you will pay, whether you are personally liable for debts if the business fails, and the kind of records you have to keep. There are other implications too so it is essential to get some objective advice before deciding, from a business adviser, accountant and/or solicitor.

If you choose any of the first three types of business (sole trader, partnership or LLP) you must register as self-employed with Her Majesty's Revenue and Customs (HMRC) – see Tax section below.

Sole trader

The simplest form of business is to operate as a sole trader, working on your own and invoicing clients directly for your services. You could be a decorator, consultant, gardener, writer, plumber, trainer, artist, dressmaker – the list is endless.

Partnership

You could go into business as a partner with another person or a number of people. Partners share the responsibilities of running the business and the profits it makes. They are all 'jointly and severally liable' for debts that the business incurs, which means that if your partners do not pay their share of the debts, either because they don't have the money or they refuse to pay, you could be liable for it all.

For this reason, and because business can throw up many potential areas for disagreement, you should be very careful about who you go into partnership with. I have heard so many people say things like: 'We've been friends for years. I know him/her inside out; they'll never let me down. No point in thinking about problems before we even start; we'll just deal with things as they come up'.

Those kind of comments always made my heart sink. Discussing all the ramifications of being in partnership and signing a partnership agreement before taking the plunge will shed light on how you each think about topics such as money, time off and individual responsibilities. What will you do if one of you wants to leave? Who has responsibility for the bank account? Who bails you out if the business is losing money? It's not pleasant to think about these possibilities at such a hopeful time, and they may never happen, but far better now than trying to do it when you're under pressure. A solicitor can provide objective help to resolve all these potentially contentious issues and will draw up a written agreement so all parties know exactly where they stand. And if you can't agree at this stage, working together is obviously not a good idea.

A Builder's Story

Nick set up a building firm in partnership with an old friend from school. He had known Paul for years, respected his standard of work, and it seemed that they had a good chance of being successful. At the outset they agreed verbally that Nick would take slightly more money out of the business each month to reimburse him for doing the books and the marketing. They had only been working together for a few months when Paul started to query this arrangement and to suggest that Nick was taking more out of the business than he was due. The situation escalated until one day Paul walked out, saying he was being ripped off, and leaving Nick in the middle of a large job with no help. Nine months later the pair are still not speaking and there is no sign of a reconciliation.

Limited Liability Partnership (LLP)

A limited liability partnership is a similar structure to a partnership, but the liability of each partner is limited to the amount of money they have put into the business, so it is not as financially risky if the business gets into trouble.

Limited Company

The fourth alternative is to 'incorporate' your business at Companies House and run it as a limited company, in which case the company is a legal entity in its own right and you are a director and employee of the company. This means that you are not personally responsible for business debts, but there are many legal responsibilities that go with being a director including the filing of company accounts and annual returns at Companies House every year.

TAX

You need to register with Her Majesty's Revenue and Customs within three months of becoming self-employed (or risk a £100 penalty), and inform them if you are setting up a limited company. I'd suggest that you make contact as soon as you're thinking of starting a business, as free workshops on how to deal with your tax are run throughout the country by Revenue staff and it's good to understand your obligations as soon as possible. Leaflets are available for people in certain types of business and 'particular occupations' whose earnings may be erratic or are dealt with differently by HMRC.

Sole traders and partnerships are required to complete a tax self-assessment form each year, while the tax for limited companies is more complex and requires a qualified accountant. The main thing to remember is that you need to put money aside throughout the year in order to pay your annual tax bill in two stages in January and July.

NATIONAL INSURANCE

You pay National Insurance contributions, also administered by HMRC, to cover your State pension and other benefits. As an employee, your employer deducts it before you receive your salary, but as a self-employed person you are responsible for paying it yourself. When you register as self-employed you start paying Class 2 National Insurance contributions on a monthly or quarterly basis. If your profit reaches a certain level, you also pay Class 4 contributions, which are a percentage of your annual profit.

VAT

Value Added Tax is a tax on certain goods and services supplied in the UK. You are required to register for VAT if your taxable turnover exceeds a certain threshold (£67,000 per annum in the tax year 2008–9). You may also register voluntarily if your turnover is less than the threshold. Once registered, you must add the appropriate tax rate to your invoices, the standard rate being 15% until the end of 2009, and you can claim back the VAT you have paid on the goods and services you buy for your business.

The VAT man is perhaps the most feared bureaucrat for those in business as he has far-reaching powers if you do not keep your affairs in order. If you keep your accounts in order and file returns on time the process is quite straightforward and there is absolutely nothing to fear. In fact, I have always found being registered for VAT a distinct blessing, as it makes me keep my books up to date.

HEALTH AND SAFETY

Health and safety laws apply to the self-employed and all businesses, no matter how small, and if you employ staff it's likely you will need to register with the Health and Safety Executive or your Local Authority. You are required to complete a risk assessment to find out the risks involved in carrying out your work and to put sensible measures in place to control them. Risks include trailing computer and telephone cables that people might trip over, hazardous substances (including cleaning materials), working on ladders, lifting, the use of computers, electrical appliances and vehicles, and stress. So you can see that nobody and no occupation can claim to be exempt. Employers with five staff or more must have a written health and safety policy.

DATA PROTECTION

Under the Data Protection Act 1998, any business that stores personal information, such as the names, addresses and other personal details about its staff or customers, should check to find out if it needs to register as a data controller with the Information Commissioner's Office (ICO).

EMPLOYING STAFF

Taking on staff is a big step for most small businesses and has the potential to make or break you. There is a massive amount of legislation relating to the recruitment, payment, discipline and firing of staff. I would therefore suggest that before taking somebody on, you find out about your legal obligations as an employer, and think very carefully about how much it will cost you in both money (wages, National Insurance, holiday pay, maternity pay etc.) and time (interviews, training, supervision, sick leave etc.).

ENVIRONMENT

The impact of all business activities on the environment has rapidly become a big issue over the last few years, and so you need to find out what the legal obligations are for your industry. This is a piece of red tape no business owner should object to – when you conserve resources and minimise waste, not only do you stay on the right side of the law, but you could save money and gain a PR advantage as well.

Managing your finances when you're self-employed

While working as a business adviser I found that employed people often regard self-employment as a licence to print money, but strangely enough that's a view never shared by the self-employed themselves! It's common for those beginning self-employment to underestimate the length of time required to start generating income from their new business. I'd suggest you have enough money to pay your bills for at least six months as there are enough pressures at this time without adding financial worries to the pot.

A Clinical Psychologist's Story

Susan was featured earlier in this chapter, talking about how her experience of the first year of running a private practice from home was in many ways more of a challenge than she had anticipated. She feels she was naïve about many things at the outset, money being one of them: 'I didn't realise how long it would take for a new business to start earning money. I'm lucky in that I had a financial buffer, but still it was scary to be chipping away at my savings. I'd wake up in a cold sweat at four in the morning, thinking "What on earth have I done? I've given up a secure job and now I've got no money coming in."'

THE FINANCIAL IMPLICATIONS OF GOING IT ALONE

It is often assumed that there are generous tax breaks for the self-employed, and conveniently forgotten that they have to cover all their costs (premises, travel, stock and materials, wages etc.) before earning any money for themselves. From the income left over you need to set aside enough for tax, National Insurance, insurances and a private pension as well as the usual living expenses (mortgage or rent, bills, food, clothes, spending money).

If you are a sole trader, it's likely no money will come in if you're not working, which means you need to earn enough over the course of the year to cover your holidays and possible sickness.

An Illustrator's View

Margaret has been a self-employed illustrator of children's books for many years and this is her perspective on being self-employed: 'I believe there's no doubt that a self-employed person is generally worse off financially than their employed equivalent, but that self-employed people do occasionally have opportunities, which employed people don't have, to earn significantly more money.'

I think it's the prospect of those opportunities that attracts many people into self-employment, and their scarcity that sends some back into employment. Bearing that in mind, think about the longer-term implications of becoming self-employed, not just over this year and next. Taking into account the lack of benefits like sick pay, holiday pay and pension schemes, you could be approaching retirement considerably worse off than if you stayed in employment all your life. A sobering thought, certainly, but the fact is that people tend to choose self-employment because it provides them with so much extra satisfaction, to the point where the financial considerations are actually secondary. If finances are most important to you, then you'll be much happier finding a job you like and sticking to it.

FUNDING/GRANTS

There is a bewildering and ever-changing array of funding and grants available to those setting up in business, from bursaries provided by blue chip companies to European and government money designed to help regenerate areas of economic deprivation.

Money for Nothing?

As a business adviser it was clear to me that the public perception of the amount and availability of grant monies bears little resemblance to the reality. So many times clients came to see me, because 'a guy in the pub told me I can get a grant for this' when in fact grants were no longer or had never been available for that industry or individual. I have also known cases where clients had borrowed and even spent money on the strength of getting these theoretical funds and were then either not eligible or had their applications rejected.

It's said that there's no such thing as a free lunch and there's no such thing as free money either. The application process will almost certainly require you to provide a business plan describing your projected performance in detail, backed up by the figures, and this kind of forecasting is time consuming. If there is funding available and your application is successful, you should be aware that the funding organisation now has a stake in your success and will require full details of your trading figures and estimates of future performance. You may be expected to display their logo prominently in your premises or on your literature and to participate in PR exercises to promote them. This might suit you fine; I have also known businesses to turn down funding after going through the process because they were unhappy with the associated terms and conditions.

If you are applying for start-up funds, try to find a business adviser to guide you and make sure you are providing all the information that is needed.

Applying for grants or funding

Give yourself the best chance of success by following these guidelines.

☐ Make sure you really are eligible as the 'criteria' – who can apply and the conditions they have to meet – tend to be strict, and there is no way the funding body will 'bend the rules a bit' no matter how brilliant your business idea.

☐ Read the instructions carefully and supply exactly what is requested, even if you can't see the point of it. If your application isn't complete it won't even be considered, simple as that.

☐ Don't be tempted to make up figures for sales, costs, profit etc. Yes, it is difficult to estimate when you haven't even started the business, but think hard about how much you can realistically produce, how many customers you can service in a day, how much you will need to pay somebody, and so on.

☐ Do some research to find out what your goods or service will cost to produce or deliver, how much the customer is likely to spend and what the subsequent profit will be. Search on the internet, look at what is being sold already, check the price range, talk to the customers who buy your product. The people examining the applications are fluent with figures and fabricated ones will be immediately apparent to them.

☐ Yes, this is all a lot of hard work, but it's supposed to be – this organisation may be handing over a wad of cash and they want to be sure you are serious about this and won't waste it. Would you give money to a friend on the basis of a whimsical idea if they weren't prepared to do some legwork to better their chances of success?

LOANS

In the boom years of the late 1990s and early 2000s the banks were flashing cash around, but the credit crunch that started in 2007 has made it more difficult to obtain loans, at least at reasonable interest rates. This might actually be all to the good of new businesses for whom the first few years are the riskiest, as it's tempting to take out a loan to finance stock, tools, premises, and so on in the high spirits of a new start. By renting, borrowing or making do you could reduce your exposure to risk.

If you do decide to apply for a loan, make doubly sure your figures stack up, if necessary by getting professional help, and that you have some leeway between income and outgoings. And definitely don't fall into the trap of inflating your sales figures so that, in theory, you can cover loan repayments. If you can't keep up your projected level of turnover and fall behind, you might also fall behind with payments to the bank and risk going bust.

INSURANCE

There is insurance available for every eventuality you can possibly think of, but when starting a business you are usually looking to keep costs to a minimum. Certain kinds of business insurance are a legal requirement however, so find out what applies to your own circumstances. Public liability insurance, for example, covers you in case you cause damage to anyone or anything in the course of your work. If you employ staff, you must have employers' liability insurance.

You may also want to cover the most basic risks to yourself and the business. As we've seen, self-employed people can't afford to be ill, so if you can afford it, look at a private health insurance that will get you into hospital and back to work quickly. A Permanent Health Insurance policy will cover your earnings if you are unable to work for an extended period of time, normally at least three months. Check the small print carefully on all policies to make sure they cover exactly what you need or the policy may not pay out when you claim.

Useful people to know when you're setting up a business

Running a business can be a lonely experience and I strongly recommend you build a carefully chosen network of people who can advise and help you. You should concentrate on your own area(s) of expertise (usually those that bring in the most revenue) and rely on others to provide specialist help. This means being very discerning in your choice of advisers.

Other people's recommendations are useful, but remember that you and your business are unique, and the person who is invaluable to an acquaintance may be less helpful to you. If you feel the slightest bit uncomfortable with a prospective adviser, they aren't the right person for you. You must be able to ask them what to you feel like stupid questions and know that you will always get a straightforward and understandable reply. The best advisers will inspire you to achieve much more than you ever would alone. (Also see Chapter 7 for how to build your own informal and formal support networks.)

BUSINESS ADVISER

I can speak on this subject from all sides of the fence, having used enterprise agency advisers at no charge, paid for advice on a private basis, and then become a business adviser myself, firstly in the private and then the public sector.

I would recommend that, as soon as you have some idea about the kind of business you wish to start, you find your nearest Business Link or enterprise agency office and ask what kind of help is available to you. If there is free advice available, make an appointment and go along. The business adviser will at the very least provide a variety of contacts and information, and at best turn out to be instrumental in getting your business off the ground. They can advise you on what other advisers you need or refer you to specialist organisations that can help you further. The Prince's Trust, for example, has a great record of providing financial and mentor support to people aged 18 to 30 who are unemployed or underemployed but want to start their own business. PRIME help people over 50 years old to do the same.

A business adviser will be able to help you come up with a business plan, which is a way of putting some flesh on the bare bones of your business idea. You need to think realistically about how much business you are likely to do, how much your costs will be, how much profit you will make, the processes and time involved, whether you need to employ anyone, and so on. Sometimes the results can be unexpected – that apparently wonderful idea doesn't generate any profit after all – and you will have to rethink. But it is so much better to do it now before you have put in all the energy and investment. You can find outline business plans on the internet or in the information packs provided by the banks for new businesses, but an adviser can interpret some of the business language for you.

Once your business is established and you have had time to learn the ropes, you might consider going back to the same business adviser to see if there is any further help they can give, or you might find a private adviser or consultant who will charge you an hourly or monthly fee to help you with a specific challenge, such as expanding your turnover.

An Objective Viewpoint

While running my cleaning business I attended a course on business finance run by my local enterprise agency and was impressed by the course leader, Michael, who turned out to be a freelance small business adviser. I agreed with Michael to pay a fixed fee each month for an agreed number of hours' face-to-face discussion and for his availability on the phone if I had a pressing problem between our sessions. It was a good investment that gave me the objective viewpoint of an experienced businessman not involved in my business on a day-to-day basis. Knowing I had backup gave me confidence in my decisions and the management of my staff. In the end Michael actually worked himself out of a job, as it was through our regular discussions that I realised I had no interest in growing the business and that it was time to sell up and do something else.

ACCOUNTANT

There is no obligation to employ an accountant as a self-employed person or small business owner, as you can do your own accounts and fill out your own annual tax returns. To my mind, however, unless you have a very low turnover, an accountant will probably pay for themselves by identifying where you can claim tax allowances to offset your tax bill. For example, it's possible to claim part of your household expenses if you are using space in your house to run the business, and there will be other allowances specific to your trade or profession.

But even if you use an accountant, it's wise to also have a basic understanding of how to put together your accounts and how to read them, so that you can ask appropriate questions about the financial performance of your business and what you could do better. My experience has been that, unless you are lucky, accountants only answer the questions they are asked and tend not to volunteer information.

BANK MANAGER

It pays to shop around for your business bank account. High street banks offer free or cheap banking to new businesses for a set period of time, but you may be able to negotiate a longer period than advertised. You may have to pay bank charges if you exceed a certain number of transactions a month, so try to estimate how many deposits and withdrawals you will be making.

Internet or postal accounts can be operated free of charge, but this is because they give you no counter service in a branch, so think about whether this will suit you and your business. For example, if you have lots of domestic customers who pay you in cash, which you then need to bank, this kind of account is unsuitable. It will be fine if you are paid by cheque or bank transfer.

Remember that bank managers are employed to make profits for their employer, not to advise you completely impartially on the best way to run your business. You will have an easier time if you can find a bank manager who is enthusiastic about your business and believes in your ability to succeed, so look for someone who responds to your idea. However, it's common for bank staff to be regularly transferred to other branches or other duties, so also be prepared for a change of face.

SOLICITOR

If you are simply becoming self-employed, there's no requirement for you to see a solicitor, but I'd definitely recommend it if you are setting up a partnership with one or more other people – see the section on Partnership above.

If you have decided that incorporation as a limited company is the way to go, you might also want to involve a solicitor, but it's not essential. As always, ask for advice.

COACH OR MENTOR

A coach is useful if you feel you could achieve more with the input of an objective outsider who can help you assess your opportunities and challenges, motivate you to do difficult things you might normally put off doing, and inspire you to tackle challenges you would otherwise find too intimidating. It's essential for you have a good working relationship with a coach so if necessary speak to several before making up your mind.

A mentor is someone with greater experience than you who has already achieved a measure of success and is willing to give you a helping hand. You can probably think of someone in your industry whom you respect and feel you could learn from. Start by inviting them out for a coffee and a chat, and see how the relationship develops.

PROFESSIONAL / INDUSTRY ASSOCIATION

Depending on your chosen business, your activities may be regulated by an association in terms of entry requirements, ongoing training, licences, certification, complaints procedures, and so on. You will normally be required to pay an annual subscription to join once entry requirements are met, but this is often a good investment. Professional associations often offer their members discounts on insurance and cheap or free legal advice. Membership can give you benefits such as the right to display the association logo on your literature, which gives you credibility in your customers' eyes, and opportunities to network with other people in the industry.

Resources

- ☐ www.berr.gov.uk/employment/employment-legislation/employment-guidance/page35663.html
  Detailed guidelines from the Department for Business Enterprise and Regulatory Reform on the right for employees to request, and duty for employers to consider, flexible working.

- ☐ www.workingfamilies.org.uk
  The Family Zone of this website provides help with thinking about flexible working, which could include working from home.

- ☐ www.homeworking.com
  This comprehensive homeworking website gives advice on spotting a scam and case studies of all kinds including network marketing.

☐ www.motheratwork.co.uk
   Check out the list of employers with a good record of supporting employees' work/life balance and register to view the latest job vacancies.

☐ *The Work We Were Born to Do: Find the Work You Love, Love the Work You Do* by Nick Williams. Element Books, 2000.
   This bestseller has helped many people find the courage to move from a job that merely paid the bills to work that is meaningful and fulfilling. If for you that also means starting your own business, have a look at Nick's website www.inspired-entrepreneur.com and download a free e-course that covers some of the key points in the book.

☐ *The E-Myth Revisited: Why Most Small Businesses Don't Work and What To Do About It* by Michael Gerber. Harper Collins, 1994.
   American Michael Gerber has worked with small businesses for many years and distilled his experiences into this book. It's unfortunate that I didn't discover it until after I had sold my cleaning business as every single episode he described happened to me. Read this before you start and pave your way to a less painful experience of small business.

☐ *The Small Business Start-up Workbook: A Step-by-step Guide to Starting the Business You've Dreamed of* by Cheryl D. Rickman. How To Books, 2005.
   This is a workbook, which means there are practical exercises scattered among the business and inspirational stuff so that you actually make progress towards getting your business up and running. There are also some fascinating insights from successful entrepreneurs about the mistakes they have made and what failure taught them.

☐ www.thebfa.org
   Almost half of the franchises operating in the UK are members of the British Franchise Association. Go to their website for comprehensive information on choosing a reputable franchise.

☐ www.dsa.org.uk
   The Direct Selling Association regulates network marketing in the UK and their website is a great resource for anyone thinking of becoming involved. You can check here whether the company you are looking at is a member of the DSA and thus bound by their strict code of ethics.

☐ www.businesslink.gov.uk
   The Business Link website is an excellent starting point if you are thinking of setting up a business. It provides links to sources of help on all the subjects

covered here, and interactive tools to help you decide what steps to take next.

☐ www.smallbusinessadvice.org.uk
Submit an enquiry to a business adviser online and find your local Enterprise Agency.

☐ www.cobwebinfo.com
Free help and advice on small business issues and the opportunity to buy reasonably priced guides and factsheets on starting a huge range of businesses.

☐ www.companieshouse.gov.uk
This is the organisation you deal with if your business becomes a limited company.

☐ www.hmrc.gov.uk
The website of Her Majesty's Revenue and Customs, or tax and VAT to the rest of us. Here you can download information and forms about tax, VAT, National Insurance and employing staff. You can also find out where to get help locally.

☐ www.hse.gov.uk
The Health and Safety Executive website where you can search for information by industry and subject and follow a step-by-step guide for those starting out.

☐ www.ico.gov.uk
The website of the Information Commissioner's Office where you can find more information about handling personal information and if necessary, register as a data controller.

☐ www.princes-trust.org.uk
The Prince's Trust can provide help for young people wishing to start a business.

☐ www.primeinitiative.org.uk
If you are over 50 years old and want to start a business, there may be help available here.

☐ www.lawsociety.org.uk/choosingandusing/helpyourbusiness/foryour business.-law
The Lawyers for your Business scheme offers a free half-hour initial consultation with a solicitor who belongs to the scheme, to assess your situation and estimate likely costs should you wish to proceed.

Part 2
Making it Happen

4

HOW DO I CREATE MY PERFECT WORKSPACE?

The great thing about making your own workspace at home is that you can say goodbye to standardised grey cubicles and workstations, and make your home office reflect your personality and interests so that you feel inspired and uplifted whenever you are working.

This chapter covers:

1. Factors to think about before starting to make a workspace at home, or when improving your existing workspace.

2. Deciding whether you are going to invite clients and other associates into your home.

3. Alternative venues if you don't want to hold meetings at home.

Setting up or improving your workspace

There are a great many factors you might wish to consider before deciding where and how to make your workspace, and they are listed below. Some of them – geographical location for example – may not be something you can change, but it will be an important factor if you are planning a complete life overhaul like some of the people in this book, and moving home as well as out of the office. All of the factors below are equally applicable to both employees and the self-employed.

DOES MY CHOSEN LOCATION SUPPORT HOMEWORKING AND MY FAMILY?

For a number of years there has been a migration of people away from cities and their stressful living conditions to the provinces and rural areas, where daily life is perceived to be calmer and more pleasant. If you are able to work from home, you might be thinking of moving out of the city, especially if you have children to consider.

Many city-dwellers dream of the good life in the country and that often includes a house surrounded by rolling fields, but think hard before making such a move. Have you and the other members of your family ever lived in a rural area, not counting a couple of weeks in a holiday cottage in summer? How will your daily life be affected if there is no handy post office or printshop around the corner? Can you do your work properly and efficiently if every small errand is a drive away?

Not So Idyllic, After All

‘ *When I began work on this book we lived in a pretty cottage in a hamlet in mid-Cornwall. Just across the road was an off-road cycle trail that led down into the nearest market town and, in the other direction, onto miles of trails across open countryside. Sounds great, the perfect combination of working from home and regular exercise. But in reality, working from home in that environment made us feel cut off from the rest of the world going about its daily routine, and we got tired of having to get in the car every time we needed to post a parcel, buy a paper or get some shopping. We decided to relocate to a small town where we can walk to the bank, library, and market. And we're not alone – estate agents report house prices are holding up better in small country towns as people seek a sense of community and easily accessible local facilities.* ’

Think about how you spend a typical day, and if you normally like to pick up your paper at the newsagent's in the morning, buy a few bits and pieces at the supermarket at lunchtime and have a stroll around the block when you need a breather, you probably need these facilities to be accessible to your home office as well.

IS THE INFRASTRUCTURE ADEQUATE?

Similarly you need to check that the infrastructure of the area supports you in working from home. Despite the widespread and increasing reliance on broadband, we all need to have face-to-face meetings sometimes, and good road, rail and air links can help you to arrive in good shape. Plus plane and rail tickets can often get you around much more cheaply than your own car, now that petrol is a significant expense.

WHAT ARE THE LEGALITIES RELATED TO MAKING A WORKSPACE AT HOME?

As we saw in Chapter 3, the fact that you are working from home doesn't mean there are no rules governing your activities. You will save yourself a lot of inconvenience and expense if you check out the following areas before setting up your home office.

Mortgage provider or landlord

If you own your home and intend to run a business from it, you should check your title deeds in case there are any restrictive covenants relating to commercial use. You should also tell your mortgage company that you are planning to work from home.

If you rent your home, you need to check your tenancy agreement as the tenancy may be for residential use only. Landlords generally don't object if you are working from home rather than running a business, but are likely to object to the use of the house for anything other than admin. work. This means that you will not be able to have business visitors at home.

Insurance

Remember to tell your insurance company that you are going to be working from home or your policies for buildings and contents insurance may become invalid and not pay out if you claim. Normally the company will want to know whether you will be having frequent visitors or if you will be keeping valuable stock and equipment on the premises. If not, they may simply alter the wording of your policy and not charge any extra premium.

If you do use expensive tools or materials, insurance is one of the first things you should consider when setting up at home.

Health and safety

Even if you are working alone, you still have a duty to keep yourself safe, so don't forget all those office rules about trip hazards like trailing cables, sticking-out drawers and fraying carpets. If you have visitors to your home office or people working with you, you should carry out a risk assessment of your activities, which means you should identify all the risks inherent in carrying out the work you do, and take practical measures to prevent them happening.

If you are an employee your employer will probably ask you to carry out your own risk assessment and arrange for Portable Appliance Testing (PAT) for your computer and any other electrical appliances you use. Each appliance must be certified every year.

Planning permission

If building work is required to accommodate your new workspace in the house or out in the garden, remember to check what permissions are needed from your local authority before starting work.

If you are running a business rather than just working from home, you should also check with the local authority that you are allowed to do so in a residential area, particularly if the business will make any noise, smells or have visiting traffic. Don't assume that you can just go ahead on the quiet; many a business has been closed down following a complaint by a disgruntled neighbour to the council. If your business involves the preparation of food you must inform the environmental health department of your local authority.

WHAT SHOULD I TELL MY NEIGHBOURS?

You may not be generating any noise or other antisocial side-effect but it's wise to tell the neighbours about your plans now rather than have your work life disrupted later if they are unhappy. Neighbours tend to get most agitated about visitors taking up precious parking spaces, but they may also be delighted that you are going to be in all day and so enhancing the security of the neighbourhood.

HOW MUCH ROOM WILL I NEED?

You will need enough room for at least a desk, chair, storage and whatever area your work demands, not forgetting to leave enough space for you to open drawers, gain easy access to sockets, change supplies in your printer, and so on.

If you are starting a business it's a good idea to think positive and allow room for expansion – storage of files, extra equipment – so that you won't have to make major changes again in a few months.

> **Just a thought:**
> Information relating to your tax returns must be kept for at least six years if you are self-employed and this includes receipts, copies of invoices, cheque and paying-in books, bank and credit card statements etc. All this paper can become very bulky so allow space on shelves or in your filing cabinet.

If you work for someone else you are bound to accumulate lots of paper and other things which will need to be stored. An employer may want to inspect the area in which you plan to work, and might refuse permission for you to work from home if they believe the space and conditions will not allow you to work safely.

WHERE SHALL I PUT MY WORKSPACE?

When deciding where to put your workspace, assuming you are in the privileged position of having a choice, look at the space already available in your house and garden and how you can adapt it for use as a home office.

Think about what your work will actually involve on a day-to-day and occasional basis, not just the bit spent sitting at a desk. If you need to keep a lot of heavy supplies or equipment, or if your work involves moving heavy objects – sofas and chairs, if you upholster furniture, for example – then that spare bedroom on the first floor may not be an ideal place. Your options will probably include:

- ☐ the kitchen or dining table

- ☐ a corner of the living room

- ☐ a landing or under the stairs

☐ a spare bedroom

☐ the attic/loft

☐ the garage

☐ an extension or separate garden room.

SHOULD MY WORKSPACE BE IN A SEPARATE ROOM?

I'm always reading in articles about working from home that it's essential to have a door you can close to keep your home office separate from the rest of the house, so you can work in peace and quiet, and then close it behind you and forget about work once the working day is over. That may be the ideal for many people, but the beauty about homeworking is that it can reflect your personality as much as you want it to, and we are all different.

A Charity Campaigner's Story

Clayton works as a part-time campaigner for a national charity and has a notably laidback approach to working from home. Initially he did try to set up a separate office in the house, but soon found it just made him feel cut off from the activities of the rest of the household, when his preference is to remain integrated while working. He likes to stay available to his young son as he works and so moved back onto the living room table. He is happy to take the odd quarter of an hour if his son needs him and makes up the time later in the evening if necessary. Clayton finds this flexible approach works best for him even if it means finishing off work at midnight.

The problem with working in the midst of the household is that you might have to keep clearing your work away at dinnertime or when you have visitors. To avoid this you could arrange the furniture to partition off your working corner, or use a screen so that you're not staring at your desk all evening. Or you could invest in one of those wardrobe-like pieces of furniture that open out to reveal a desk and space for a computer and can be completely closed up when you finish work.

IS A HOUSE WITH A DEDICATED WORKSPACE WORTH MORE?

Consider the impact your changes are likely to make on the value of your house and make sure you are adding value, not making an eccentric permanent change which suits you but will put off a future buyer. A well planned home office will be a positive factor to many buyers and may well add value. An estate agent will be able to advise you on the best changes to make to enhance the appeal and value of your house, so consult one before undertaking significant changes.

WHAT ABOUT THE HEATING AND LIGHTING?

You need pleasant working conditions in your home office or the quality of your work will suffer. Bear in mind that you can get very cold sitting still at a computer for hours in winter, or very hot without any ventilation in the summer, so you need adequate, adjustable heating and a source of fresh air, ideally a window you can gaze out of when in need of inspiration.

A window also gives you natural light, which is the best and most relaxing on the eye. If you need artificial lighting, make sure it is even and doesn't reflect off your computer screen.

DO I NEED TO BUY NEW FURNITURE?

Tempting as it is to go on a shopping spree when setting up your workspace, it's not necessary to spend lots of money and anyway you might be on a strict budget if you're setting up a business. It may be possible to use furniture you already have, but do balance that against the need to feel comfortable and have your back properly supported when you are working. It's not a good idea to buy office furniture without trying it for size first. You're going to be spending many hours using it and it has to feel comfortable.

A good compromise would be to buy secondhand office furniture from a dealer who buys up excess stock and cleans it up. That way you get properly designed pieces at a competitive price and you can feel you're doing your bit for the environment. You can find outlets in Yellow Pages or the local paper.

The amount of furniture and equipment an employer provides you with will probably be in proportion to the number of hours you spend working from home.

Just a thought:

if your employer is going to supply you with office furniture, measure your chosen space carefully, allowing plenty of room for manoeuvre, as conventional office furniture is often too large to be accommodated in a domestic setting, particularly in new houses.

If you are buying new furniture, look at the ranges available from domestic furniture retailers, as these are designed to fit into the home.

Desk

Your desk should be big enough to allow you to write on an A4 pad and move documents around, as well as accommodate your screen, keyboard and speakers. A matt surface is less tiring on the eye.

Chair

Choose a swivel chair on castors if you spend a fair amount of time at your desk, as it's much less tiring than pushing back a normal chair and you can spin round to get things out of your cabinet. Five spokes at the base will be more stable than four. Check the chair is adjustable in height and tilt and that it supports your back. Use a footrest if you can't comfortably rest your feet on the floor and if you have back problems, look for an ergonomic or kneeling chair. Arm rests can be a nuisance if they stop you rolling the chair under the desk.

Storage

You'll need some kind of storage to keep papers and bits and pieces in order. I like to keep as much as possible out of sight or I get demoralised by the thought of all the work that remains to be done. Traditional office filing cabinets eat up piles of paper and their deep drawers will hide away small bits of equipment. You might need lockable drawers and a shredder to comply with an employer's confidentiality policy.

HOW SHOULD I ORGANISE MY WORKSPACE?

Unless you are lucky enough to have a very large area for your new workspace, most rooms already have factors like doors, windows, radiators and electrical sockets that limit where you can place your furniture and equipment. This can actually be a benefit, as it gives you a starting point around which to fit everything, whereas a completely blank canvas can be bewildering. Using your workspace is the only way to find out whether it is practical and efficient, so treat your first layout as a trial run and tell yourself you will change it round if it doesn't work well for you. This is much less demoralising than feeling you've got it wrong and have to start all over again.

SPACE-SAVING IDEAS

Space is usually at a premium in home offices so get the most out of the room available to you with these space-saving ideas:

☐ A small pedestal cabinet on castors can be rolled neatly underneath a desk or used as a surface for a printer.

☐ Put your printer or scanner on top of the filing cabinet – if not used, this is a space that often gathers junk.

☐ Consider having a laptop as your main computer. It saves desk space and gives you all-important mobility.

☐ Buy multi-function machines that copy, print, fax and scan, to save space, electrical sockets and money.

□ Fix your phone and desk lamp on the wall to save space. A low, wide shelf will hold a printer where there's no room for a piece of furniture.

□ Get a joiner to shape a piece of timber or worktop to fit into an oddly shaped space like a corner or alcove.

WHO PAYS FOR THE RUNNING EXPENSES OF MY WORKSPACE?

As a self-employed person you will be able to claim against tax for a proportion of the running costs of your house. But do seek advice on this from an accountant to make sure you're not hit with a capital gains bill from the taxman when you sell your house.

It's likely an employer would take the view that any costs incurred through working from home will be offset by your savings on commuting, and they may therefore be unwilling to contribute to the costs of heating and lighting your home office.

WHAT ABOUT THE IT SIDE OF THINGS?

Sockets

Calculate how many electrical sockets you need for your computer, printer, scanner, fax etc. and add on a few more for future requirements. If necessary, get more sockets installed rather than overload the system by plugging lots of appliances into an adaptor. If you are starting from scratch you could consider putting sockets above desk level, rather than just above the skirting board, so you can reach them easily.

Phone

You may need at least one more phone socket for internet use and while you're putting that in, it's worth debating whether to get separate phone lines for home and business. The advantage of separate lines is that you always know how to answer when the phone rings, a formal business reply or an informal hello, and you might want to ban the kids from answering the business line. (See also Chapter 6 on maintaining a professional image.)

A Financial Adviser's Story

Rhodri is a financial adviser who used to work from a spare bedroom and could never resist answering the business line out of working hours, although he knew he should have been relaxing. He now has a self-contained office on a lower floor of his house and, although the domestic phone line is accessible in both the house and office, the business phone is out of earshot when he has finished work, a situation he finds much more conducive to relaxation.

Computer

Your job will dictate whether you use a PC or Mac, and space whether you stick to a laptop. When using a computer, the Health and Safety Executive (HSE) recommends that your forearms should be roughly horizontal and your eyes at the same height as the top of your screen. You should be able to use your mouse with a relaxed arm and straight wrist, and get up for regular breaks to rest your body and eyes.

The HSE advises that it's better to take regular short breaks than a longer one less often. For example they suggest a five to ten minute break every hour in preference to 20 minutes every two hours.

Just a thought:
If you are the kind of person who likes to be in company, buy the smallest and lightest laptop you can find so you can go out at the drop of a hat to work in a coffee shop or some other busy place.

Your employer is likely to have rules on whether you can use their equipment for personal use or allow other people to use it. In Chapter 8 there is a cautionary tale about a child's use of his homeworking mum's computer.

Broadband

Broadband is now available almost everywhere in the UK but it's worth checking that you can get it and what the speed is. If you have more than one computer you can get them networked together, either hardwired or wireless (although there has been negative publicity about the health implications of wireless networks).

If someone is working with you, or your children will be playing computer games at the same time as you're working, you will lose a lot of your bandwidth, so consider having two broadband connections if the bandwidth is insufficient to support both activities. You can get broadband for home or business use. Home use is cheaper, but you share the bandwidth with more people. Before signing up, check whether there are limits on how much you can download, as your ration may be quickly used up if your children are downloading games and videos.

IT support

It will pay dividends to find a competent and reasonably priced computer engineer now rather than waiting until something goes wrong. And what about backing up your work? IT experts recommend you keep a back-up off-site in case of an emergency like a fire. Your stress levels benefit from having contingencies in place to deal with such crises, even if you never need to use them, so have a look at Chapter 9 too.

HOW CAN I RUN A GREEN WORKSPACE?

There are undoubted benefits for the environment in large numbers of people working from home and cutting out the commute, but you might be thinking that your own energy use and utility bills will be shooting up if you're at home all day long. You can offset the expense to some extent by claiming for a proportion of your household bills when you do your tax return, and you might also want to check how well your house is insulated and glazed.

Save money, save the environment

Here are more ways of cutting down your household and business bills and doing your bit for the planet:

- ☐ Turn off the light when you are not in your workspace, and switch off and unplug office machinery at night if it has a stand-by function or it will still draw energy that you have to pay for.

- ☐ Turn off your monitor when you have a break.

- ☐ If possible, print on both sides of paper and tear up mistakes to use as scrap.

- ☐ Look for the Print This Page button when printing from the internet, or cut and paste only the required information into a Word document.

- ☐ Reduce margin sizes and font size to get more on a page, and use the Print in Grayscale/Black Cartridge Only and Fastdraft facilities whenever appropriate. (This can be found with the print properties button in the print window of your computer.)

- ☐ Recycle your shredded paper or put it in the compost bin.

- ☐ Recycle printer cartridges and mobile phones as well as paper, cardboard and plastic bottles.

- ☐ When using a new folder, stick a white label on it and write the subject in pencil. When the project is complete, rub out the name and start again.

- ☐ Boil a cup or mugful of water for your coffee, not the whole kettle.

- ☐ Fix a thermostatic valve to the radiator in your workspace so you can adjust the heating independent of the rest of the house.

Just a thought:
Homeworkers often don't feel justified in putting on the central heating when they are the only one at home all day, so some form of portable heating will keep you from freezing.

☐ Send e-cards at Christmas. We did it with great trepidation two years ago and the response from clients and associates was overwhelmingly positive. Donate the amount you save on cards and postage to your favourite charity – it soon mounts up.

DECORATION

This is the fun part – now that all the red tape and physical requirements are sorted out, you can make your workspace an enjoyable place to be. It doesn't have to look like an office at all, although bear in mind the impression it might make if you ever have visitors.

You can paint or paper the walls in your favourite colours and patterns and put up the paintings, posters and photos that invigorate and inspire you. It's a good idea to display mementoes of your achievements and successes, such as qualifications, certificates, awards, and letters of thanks. Seeing these around you will boost your confidence. Photos of family will remind you why you are working hard and give you an incentive when you're flagging. Buy colourful files, not those dull, institutional ones that come in packs and make everything look so boring.

Some people are inspired by having a 'dream board' over their desk, a notice board where you stick pictures of what you want to achieve, whether that be a car, a house, a holiday destination, professional recognition, a major contract, and so on. The idea is that the pictures act as a reminder to keep plugging away when the going gets tough, and being constantly in your mind, they will also attract the circumstances and people you need to achieve those things. It's got to be worth a try.

Plants are a useful addition to your workspace. Not only do they provide a shot of life and colour but they also filter pollutants from the air and increase the negative ionisation and oxygen content of air, mitigating the effects of electronic equipment and making you feel better. Peace Lilies are particularly good for this, as are philodedrons and rubber plants.

SHOULD I KEEP MY WORKSPACE PRIVATE?

Now your home workspace is set up, you and you alone can decide who comes in and when. In the next section we look at the pros and cons of having visitors to your workspace and in Chapter 8 at establishing healthy boundaries between work and home, including guidelines for children. In the meantime, here is an example of how working from home can benefit the extended family:

The New Chick in the Office

❛ *Nick and Toni publish magazines from the home office in their old farmhouse, and an assortment of pets and animals roam happily around the garden with their three children. On one of my visits I discovered Nick sharing his office with a pen containing a tiny chick that had been rejected by its mother. Our conversation was accompanied by a cheerful cheeping and pecking.* ❜

Should I invite people into my workspace?

When you work from home for someone else, you will probably work to a set of guidelines as to who may visit you at home – colleagues are usually OK – and who should not – usually clients and associates who work for other organisations. So you are spared the decision self-employed people often have to make about who, if anyone, should visit them at home.

ADVANTAGES OF HAVING MEETINGS AT HOME

☐ If you work all or most of the time at home, you may struggle to think of anywhere else to meet people.

☐ Your materials, literature, records and so on are stored at home and it would be inconvenient to transport them elsewhere.

☐ You are literally on 'home territory' and would feel out of your depth somewhere else.

☐ Your visitor might enjoy the lack of formality and getting to know your home and family. It might become a reason they do business with you.

DISADVANTAGES OF HAVING MEETINGS AT HOME

☐ You may be operating very efficiently from your kitchen table but what kind of impression is it going to create on customers or suppliers? Is it going to make you appear less professional and more of a dabbler?

☐ Your whole home and lifestyle will be under scrutiny as well as your business. Every time you have a visitor you will have to make sure the house is clean and tidy, especially if you only have an upstairs toilet and visitors need to walk through the whole house to reach it.

☐ What impact will your meetings have on other members of your family? Your spouse and/or children may resent having to stay quiet or out of sight for the duration.

- You may feel anxious throughout the meeting in case you are disturbed by family or an unexpected caller, or unsure how to handle a business meeting in the place where you usually only entertain family and friends.

- Your client may be unsure how to behave when the boundaries between a business and personal visit are blurred. They may feel under pressure to admire your décor or your children, and uncertain how to start and end the meeting.

- The level of intimacy involved in going into someone's home may be too high for some people and make them feel pressurised into doing business with you, so they opt out instead.

Blurred Boundaries

My partner occasionally used to see coaching and hypnotherapy clients at home. Fortunately we had plenty of private parking, but the house wasn't the easiest to find and sometimes clients arrived flustered or late after getting lost. The most comfortable place for Andy to see them was the sitting room, but since the obvious entrance to the house was at the side, clients would often come through the kitchen and dining room first. If they wanted to use the bathroom, they had to go upstairs. This meant we often had a frantic period of tidying before they arrived for their appointment. In addition, I either had to arrange to be out when a client was there or make sure I had organised plenty of desk work to do so I could close myself off in one of our offices upstairs where I was out of earshot.

How you decide whether or not to have all or some of your meetings at home will depend on your family circumstances, your home, the nature of your work and the adaptability of your business associates. You could try out one of the alternatives described below or think about investing in the ideal solution – a totally self-contained office complete with its own entrance – so that there's no need for your visitors to set foot in your home at all.

A Psychotherapist's Story

Tina had a therapy room upstairs in her home but when she had a bad car accident and could no longer get up the stairs, she was forced to use her sitting room. This was unsatisfactory for various reasons – there was always a risk of someone coming to the door, it was difficult for her to relax in the same space after work, and it was impossible to avoid moving things around, when a therapy room should be kept the same to allow the therapist to process changes in the client.

Tina's solution is a wooden cabin at the end of the garden, specifically designed for its purpose, equipped with electricity, heating and phone and surrounded by fields: 'I love it because now clients don't need to go into my home and I'm able to switch off much more easily now that I 'go out' to work. My clients love the cabin for its peacefulness and feeling of safety. It wasn't cheap, and it took time to think it through, but it will pay for itself in time.'

Alternatives to meeting people at home

If you decide that your circumstances are not suitable for having business visitors to your home workspace, there are a number of ways to get around it.

GO TO THEM

If you are dealing with businesses operating out of their own premises, you can avoid the issue ever arising by always suggesting that you visit them. Most people are too busy to even notice that you always go to them and will simply be glad not to have to make a journey to see you. They may never even know that you work from home.

In the case of private individuals it may be most convenient to visit them at home, if they are amenable. If you don't already know them well, make sure you take commonsense precautions to ensure your own safety.

Interviews at Home

‘ *I regularly needed to interview applicants for part-time cleaning jobs and I discovered a number of ways of dealing with the situation, each with its own advantages and drawbacks.*

One option was to visit applicants in their own homes, which gave me the advantage of seeing whether they kept their own environment clean and tidy, although this was not necessarily a good predictor of how well they would do the job. You might think that people would object to a prospective employer coming to their home, but it seemed to be a common practice of cleaning firms and nobody ever refused to let me visit.

The potential problem with this tactic was personal security. I felt happy with it if the individual had come recommended by someone I already knew, but if they were a total stranger, I would take along my cleaning supervisor, mainly for my own peace of mind, but also for her second opinion. I can only remember a couple of times when we felt uneasy, and fortunately we had already discussed how to make a quick getaway without appearing rude. ’

COFFEE SHOPS ETC.

Depending on the situation and whether or not your discussion is confidential, a coffee shop or hotel lobby may be the best place, but you will need to choose carefully bearing in mind levels of formality, privacy and noise, and how long you can decently expect to stay. Trying to shout over the clattering of crockery is tiring and unbusinesslike, while talking to a stranger in a quiet place while other customers eavesdrop is embarrassing and offputting.

If meeting someone of the opposite sex you will want to avoid any embarrassing overtones of a 'date' which might make the meeting awkward for you both and jeopardise your business relationship.

JOBCENTRE

If you are an employer recruiting through your local Jobcentre, there may be an interview room they can offer you free of charge. Availability depends on the size of the Jobcentre, so contact your local office for more details.

RENT SOME SPACE

Beauty salon/complementary health centre

If you are a therapist or counsellor of some kind, your local beauty salon or complementary health centre may have rooms available to rent for the day or half-day. Your profile will benefit from your presence on the high street and by being included in their marketing.

Rooms in cafés/restaurants/pubs/hotels

If you need to hold a meeting or interview a number of people, cafés, restaurants and pubs often have private rooms for hire for an hour or half-day. Some may charge for use of the room, others may offer it free of charge as long as you buy refreshments.

Community halls

Village and community halls are often of a high standard these days and eager to rent space to make money.

Incubation and business start-up units

Your local authority and university may have low-priced units available for start-up businesses in specified industries.

Serviced office accommodation

In many towns and cities you can rent serviced office accommodation, paying to use a desk, office or meeting room for a specified period of time and to use services such as printing, photocopying and making phone calls.

Workhubs

Business support agencies, councils and other interested parties are getting together in parts of the country to raise funding to create so-called 'workhubs' for local home-based businesses, to help them overcome the kinds of challenges we're looking at in this book. Workhubs provide a reasonably priced venue to meet clients on neutral ground, or just to get out of the house into a stimulating change of environment and network with other businesses and potential associates. Their affordability makes them the ideal next step if your business is expanding and you want to take it out of the home. Workhubs are also being used as a focal point for the delivery of business advice that might otherwise not reach businesses closeted away at home.

LIVE/WORK UNITS – THE FUTURE OF HOMEWORKING?

The concept of live/work properties is a relatively new one and one that is growing in popularity. Live/work properties are designed from the outset to accommodate both living and working space, as distinct from houses in which a spare room has been converted or added as a home office, and in which the predominant use is still domestic. Live/work units tend to have a larger proportion of space devoted to business use and may be able to accommodate employees and business growth.

A number of issues arise with the new concept of live/work properties, including getting planning permission to build them, when land use has traditionally been split into domestic and business use. Conventional financial rules are also challenged by live/work properties – some lenders are wary about live/work mortgages and put a restriction on the percentage of space that can be used for business. At the time of writing a live/work unit owner's liabilities regarding council tax, Capital Gains Tax and VAT are still far from clear-cut. If only bureaucracy was as resourceful and ready to adapt as homeworkers.

Resources

☐ www.howstuffworks.com/home-office.htm
   Articles on setting up a workspace, with up-to-date details on choosing hardware and software, equipment reviews and explanations of how photocopiers, scanners etc. work.

☐ www.insight.bt.com/Topics/Where-you-work
   BT pioneered home and flexible working long before other employers and has an obvious vested interest in its growth. The Insight website advertises its

products and services but also has good quality articles on many aspects of working from home.

☐ www.bytestart.co.uk
Click on the Office & Home link for regularly updated articles on setting up a workspace at home.

☐ www.shedworking.co.uk
Alex Johnson is a man happily obsessed with his shed and he runs 'the only daily updated guide to the lifestyles of shedworkers and those who work in shedlike atmospheres'. If you are tempted by the prospect of relocating to the end of the garden, Alex is your man. He provides photos of all kinds of sheds and an encyclopaedic listing of the suppliers of garden offices.

☐ www.businesslink.gov.uk
Click on the Health, Safety and Premises link on the left-hand menu, followed by Working Environment, for a wealth of information on working safely at home.

☐ www.workhubs.com
An introduction to the idea of workhubs and what they can achieve for home-based business, with links to successful hubs in Shrewsbury, Penzance and Dublin: www.enterprise-hq.co.uk, www.digitalpeninsula.com, www.thedigital hub.com

☐ www.liveworkhomes.co.uk
This colourful and clearly written site showcases live/work properties around the country and is packed with information about buying or renting a live/work property.

5

CAN I BE PRODUCTIVE AT HOME?

When you work with other people, you are automatically part of a dynamic system that demands your participation and provides the pressure to achieve. It's understandable that many people worry that, despite being away from the office politics and constant interruptions when you are working from home, it could be difficult to achieve anything when there is no external pressure to get your work done.

In this chapter you will:

1. Discover that homeworkers can be much more productive than their colleagues in the office.

2. Develop your own most productive style of working from home.

3. Create a structure for your day to keep you focused.

4. Become aware of common time wasters and how to avoid them.

5. Understand why you procrastinate and what you can do about it.

Productive or fat, depressed and lazy?

A survey conducted in early 2007 by Australian magazine *Home Beautiful* found that many of its readers feared working from home would make them 'fat, depressed and lazy'. A third of the people polled believed they would sit watching television and eating all day, while a fifth thought the lack of company would be demoralising.

However, almost half believed they would actually be *more* productive at home, away from the many distractions of the typical workplace, and this is indeed what BT have found – their homeworkers are on average about 20% more productive than their office-based colleagues. Even this figure, although impressive, pales into insignificance compared with results from the SusTel (Sustainable Teleworking) project by the UK Centre for Economic and Environmental Development, published in 2004. The project examined the economic, environmental and social impacts of homeworking in five European countries, including the UK.

> **It's a fact that...**
> homeworkers surveyed in the SusTel project estimated their productivity to be between 60 and 80% better than they could achieve in an office, and the quality of their work to be 57 to 77% better.

The people I spoke to when researching this book certainly believe that this is the case – higher productivity was one of the positive factors of homeworking most often mentioned. In fact many homeworkers find that, far from being unproductive, their greatest challenge is not to get too involved with work and end up working much longer hours than their office-based colleagues. When work is on the dining room table or behind the study door, it's very easy to keep working away until you have very little time left for personal and family interests, and then to pop back in after dinner or at weekends to check emails and phone messages.

A Project Manager's Story

Amina has worked at home in various managerial roles for eight years. She requested home working from her employer because she was fed up with wasting three hours on commuting every day and finds she is now 'a lot more productive, because I work a lot more at home. I can take the children to school and then start work when I get back. I carry on working while I eat lunch, pick the children up in the afternoon and then go back to work. Sometimes dinner is late on the table if I'm still busy, but I have learnt to switch the computer off and not return to it after dinner. And nowadays I never touch it at weekends.'

Traditionally employees tend to be assessed on the hours they put in at the office rather than the amount of work they get through. We've all come across the people who never do a stroke of work but somehow manage to convince management they are performing well. In a survey carried out in 2005 by America Online and Salary.com, American workers admitted wasting more than two hours of work time every day surfing the net, chatting with other staff and carrying out personal business. So just being physically present by no means ensures a high standard of productivity.

A Designer's Story

Kevin has worked at home for eight years in TV, DVD and web design. For a brief period during this time he went back to work for a creative agency in their premises. 'Having worked on my own for a while, I found it very difficult to go back to an office environment and my motivation dropped while I was there. Although I like having people around me to bounce ideas off, I didn't like having to deal with office politics again. Even knowing what to wear was a problem, as I'd become used to being really casual at home. And having had the freedom to set my own working hours, knowing that I had to be there between certain times, and be seen to be working even when I wasn't feeling particularly creative, was hard to handle.'

Finding your most productive homeworking style

I suggested in Chapter 2 that you give yourself the best possible chance of success in homeworking if you understand your personality and how you are likely to respond to the challenges of working from home. You will also make the best possible use of your time if you understand what may seem like insignificant personal quirks, such as which tasks you enjoy the most, the kind of clothes that make you feel businesslike as well as comfortable, and the time of day you are most able to concentrate and produce quality work. In order to think about your habits a little more objectively, ask yourself the questions listed below. It might help to write down your answers in a notebook and add more as you think of them. You are building up a picture of the best working pattern for you and it might take a little while to complete. Here are the questions.

WHAT TIME OF DAY ARE YOU AT YOUR BEST?

Do you wake up in the morning raring to go, or do you need several cups of coffee to ease you gently into the day, only hitting your stride by mid-morning? You might be one of those people who doesn't get creative until the evening, when the distractions of the day are over. Or do you have to be as productive as possible when the children are out at nursery? When have you recently been pleased with your work – was the time of a day a contributing factor?

A Photographer's Story

Richard runs a media company: 'I find the three hours after midnight the most productive of my day, as there are no interruptions and the London photo agencies I deal with provide a 24-hour service so there is always someone available to talk to. I usually go to bed at 4 a.m. and get up at 10 a.m. It doesn't make me particularly popular with my partner, but she works with me in the business and we see it as an investment for the family's future.'

WHAT ARE YOU GOING TO WEAR?

One of the most liberating aspects of working from home is that you no longer have to conform to a dress code and you may well save money by no longer having to buy and dry clean 'office clothes'. In theory you can now slop around in your pyjamas and dressing gown all day, although I've never met a homeworker who does, perhaps because they quickly realise that clothes have a profound effect on your mood and hence your productivity. Neil is a financial adviser who sometimes works from home. He finds that he needs to put on his suit, just as he would if he was going to the office or to visit a client, if he is to get into a businesslike frame of mind. Don't underestimate the power of clothes – notice and record how different styles make you feel. You might need to rethink your wardrobe as a homeworker, and maybe you'll need to buy some new outfits.

An Illustrator's Story

Margaret is a children's book author and illustrator who has worked from a studio at home for many years. She finds that her isolation breeds a kind of sartorial inferiority complex which makes her believe that she must be very scruffy compared to the people who work at her publisher's office, but she enjoys the change and the challenge of 'dressing up' when she goes to London to meet her publisher.

WHAT IS YOUR PREFERRED STYLE OF WORKING?

Do you need as much quiet as possible, or do you like to have the radio or a CD playing in the background to help you concentrate? Robin, a writer, starts off by working in silence but puts some rousing music on to boost his energy levels when he feels he is slowing down. Write down your own preferences. Are you one of those people who can't work when there's a discussion going on or when the songs have lyrics? Or do you just like the radio playing quietly so you don't feel entirely alone? Bear in mind that your preferences may change over time, or for different types of activity. When Liam started freelance writing at home, he put in earplugs to help him 'get in the zone'. After a while, he began to put on classical music as well as using the earplugs. He doesn't really understand the habit, just that it works for him.

WHICH JOBS COME EASILY TO YOU?

According to American motivational speaker, Brian Tracy, to be most effective, you need to 'eat that frog' first thing in the morning! In other words, if straightaway you can do the thing you find the most objectionable, the rest of the day will be easy. Which jobs are you always putting off? Try making a list of your tasks in reverse order of preference. If you can get into the habit of doing the ones at the top of your list before everything else and without too much agonising, you have the rest of the day to enjoy the remaining jobs. Use your list when creating a structure for your day, which we will come to later in the chapter.

HOW DO YOU ACTUALLY SPEND YOUR TIME?

It is easy to believe you are working hard when in fact you are spending a lot of time checking emails, surfing the net, making drinks and snacks or chatting about non-work topics.

Try making a chart which divides your day into quarter-hour chunks, like solicitors do so that they know how much to charge clients. Record on the chart how you have spent each chunk of time. Then after a week or so, check through to find out how you are really spending your time. You might be surprised how much time you are losing on unproductive activities. If you are, don't despair – read on to the sections about time management and procrastination later in this chapter. Also see Chapter 2 for how Kevin recognised he was wasting time and changed his habits to become more productive.

> **Just a thought:**
> Keep a pad of paper and a pen handy in various places around the house, and with you when you go out. Good ideas pop up at strange times and it's easy to forget them if you don't write them down straightaway.

MAKE SURE YOU ACKNOWLEDGE AND CELEBRATE YOUR SUCCESSES

You probably feel sometimes that there aren't enough hours in the day and that you are constantly running to keep up with all the changes in your industry or profession. It's easy when you've achieved something to barely acknowledge it and just keep moving on to the next target or project, especially when there's nobody around to celebrate with you. Make a point of stopping briefly to give yourself a pat on the back, maybe ring someone to tell them how pleased you are, and give yourself a treat, lunch out or a little present. Celebrating like this helps to maintain your confidence and enthusiasm and gives you something to look forward to if you're struggling to complete a task.

Creating a structure for your day and staying focused

Once you understand what makes you tick and what your preferences are, you can design a workable structure for your day. The way you organise your day may be dictated by commitments relating to children or other responsibilities, so start with considerations like the school run, and build your day around them.

USING A DIARY

As a homeworker, it's essential to have a diary, whether it's the traditional book and pen, a program on your computer or a hand-held gadget. Putting all work and domestic commitments into your diary as soon as you make them will avoid arrangements that clash. If you are just starting to work from home, you could include breaks and the time you plan to finish work. It's a good idea to note down deadlines and divide the work involved into manageable chunks with their own deadlines, so that you are working steadily towards your goal.

FITTING IN HOUSEWORK

I find that just as you probably don't have time to do much housework before leaving home to travel to work, it's best to ignore all but the quickest and most basic household tasks if your office is at home. Once started, you can easily be swept along into an hour or so of cleaning and tidying. After all, it is work of a kind and you'll feel virtuous doing it, but unfortunately it doesn't actually earn you any money.

If you are working from home and your partner goes out to work, there may be an expectation that you will do the lion's share of the housework. We look at establishing boundaries in Chapter 8, but for now just bear in mind that first thing in the morning might be a good time to ignore the household chores.

MOVING FROM HOME TO WORK

It is vital to have some kind of routine to ease the transition from home preoccupations and get the working day started. When you work away from home, the trip to work not only moves you physically to another space, it also allows your mind to switch from personal to work concerns. If work takes place at home, you need to develop another way to achieve this.

I have heard of people who get up, dress smartly, and go out to walk around the block before returning home and starting work. A friend knew a keen cyclist who would go for a morning bike ride and start work after he had had a shower. Experiment for yourself and find out what gives you the message that you should now switch into business mode. My own routine has changed many times over the years and no doubt will do so again, reflecting the different commitments I have and the fact I get bored when the same thing happens day after day. Change yours when it gets too predictable and you'll feel more energised.

A Marketing Manager's Story

Sara has a dog that needs a walk in the morning after breakfast, so the walk gives her the time to switch into working mode. When she gets home, she puts on the computer. Digby now recognises that the sound of the computer opening up signals the start of the working day and is the cue for him to settle into his basket. Sara takes a break when her teenage son returns from school and wants her attention. She prepares dinner and returns to work after the family have eaten their meal and exchanged the day's news.

STARTING YOUR DAY

So here you are at your desk or workbench, but perhaps you're still not in the mood for work. Following these steps may help.

- ☐ Always check your diary first thing so you don't miss any early phone calls or appointments. It's helpful to think now about planning your day, taking into account when you will need to stop work to prepare for a meeting or drive to pick up the kids. (See Chapter 2 'How do you keep time?' for tips on keeping tabs on time).

☐ Start your day by browsing any websites you have come across in magazine and newspaper articles or promotional material. They can be related to work or pleasure. Maybe visit the website of your favourite newspaper. If you belong to an online network (see Chapter 7), now is a good time to check for new messages in your inbox or on the forums.

☐ Check your business or personal bank accounts online. My business adviser used to say there is no excuse for not knowing exactly how much money is in your account at any time. Most of us probably don't meet these exacting standards so it's a good idea to look regularly and not be taken by surprise by a large upcoming commitment. Not to mention the motivation your current balance can supply, either because it's satisfyingly fat or worryingly slender.

☐ Look at emails next. Nikki noticed the difference when her internet went down for several weeks and her publishing company had no email to check first thing in the morning: 'It was quite difficult to get going. Emails kickstart the day. They tend to set the tone for the day and dictate what I do and what my priorities are.'

☐ Now make phone calls. Speaking to other people will motivate you and perhaps provide some deadlines or help to prioritise your work.

SETTING BREAK TIMES

You might want to set yourself break times before you even start work, just as breaks are often allocated in the workplace and strictly adhered to. Put your break times in the diary just as you do meetings and appointments. If you are an in-time person (see Chapter 2) and lose track of time, you could set your mobile or an alarm clock to ring and remind you to take a break. It is tempting to think you can just keep on working, but you will become less and less productive. Bear in mind the human brain is apparently only able to concentrate for 20 minutes at a time! I find that two hours is about the most I can manage before I feel myself starting to run out of steam.

GETTING SOME FRESH AIR

I find it essential to get out of the house at least once a day, even if it's only to pop down the road for a paper. You have the flexibility your office-bound friends are so envious of, so use it! You are now in the position to be able to combine business and pleasure – after a meeting, have lunch out, meet a friend or have a walk in the park.

Most of us are not very productive immediately after lunch, so this is a good time to have a walk and get some fresh air and a fresh perspective. It's all too easy to forget there's a whole world going on outside your workroom door. While you are out, make a point of talking to other people. In Chapter 7 we will be looking at ways of building and maintaining support networks – it's vital that you feel plugged into a larger system, or you'll grind to a halt.

TAKING NAPS

I know many people are unwilling to take naps during the day as they feel guilty about wasting time. I actually associate naps with working hard, as when I ran my cleaning business, I often had to go out early in the morning to check the office cleaning. After completing my admin. and organisation, I had a break in the afternoon before going out in the evening to see my cleaners while they were at work. I was sometimes so physically tired that an afternoon nap was essential. These days I'm not doing such physical work but I still find that a nap can be a good way to rejuvenate my brain. It gives my unconscious mind a chance to come up with an idea while my busy conscious mind is switched off. I believe that the work ethic many of us have absorbed during our upbringing can in fact have a detrimental effect on our performance. We simply cannot work all the time; we need time to absorb and assimilate information if we are to use it in the most efficient way.

> **It's a fact that...**
>
> Winston Churchill, that famous homeworker at No. 10, believed in afternoon naps and took them throughout the Second World War. 'You must sleep some time between lunch and dinner, and no half-way measures. Take off your clothes and get into bed. That's what I always do. Don't think you will be doing less work because you sleep during the day. That's a foolish notion held by people who have no imagination. You will be able to accomplish more.'
>
> Source: The Churchill Centre, transcription of a conversation in spring, 1946

EATING

What about the 'fat' part of the 'fat, depressed and lazy' fear expressed by those taking part in the Australian magazine survey on homeworking? (See the start of this chapter.) It's so easy to get up and make a coffee when work is not going well, and OK, just a few biscuits as well, and maybe a piece of that pie left over from last night.

Chapter 8 looks at ways of maintaining your weight and fitness when you are working from home. Healthy snacks are good for keeping your energy up throughout the day, so have a full and tempting fruit bowl. A handful of pumpkin seeds will provide your daily recommended amount of zinc, which helps your thinking ability and memory, and nuts are a source of Vitamin E, also linked to memory enhancement.

GETTING TIRED

It helps to recognise the symptoms that you are getting tired of a task and would benefit from a break or moving on to do something else for a while. I've noticed while writing that a recurring use of the word count button signals I am running out of inspiration and it's time to stop. If I go off and do some reading or tidy up the house, I can come back later with renewed brainpower.

ENDING YOUR DAY

You may like to set a finishing time in advance when you are planning your daily schedule, perhaps at around the time that your office-bound peers are logging off and joining the queues of commuters. Their journey home signals the end of the working day, but you may need a similar routine to your morning one – perhaps another walk with the dog or a bike ride – to emphasise that the business of the day is done and domestic concerns can now take over. Getting out of the house and putting some physical distance between you and your tools or the computer can really help you to switch off from thoughts of work.

Making the most of your time

Time management is one of the buzzwords of recent times and there is an infinite amount of information out there, in books, on the net, and in training courses. But it's very simple – when you think about it, you can't manage time at all. What you can do is manage yourself and prioritise the demands on your time. There's a famous story about this. The details vary depending where you read it, but the basic principle is the same.

THE BEST-PAID TIME MANAGEMENT TIP EVER?

In the 1930s, Charles Schwab was the head of Bethlehem Steel, America's largest independent steel producer. He asked a well known management consultant, Ivy Lee, how to increase efficiency in the company. This was Lee's advice:

1. Write down all the jobs you want to do tomorrow, and list the five most important in order of priority.

2. As soon as you start work tomorrow morning, start on the first item and don't give up until it is complete, or as complete as you are able to make it.

3. Then start on the second item. If other jobs arise during the day, only deal with them if they are more important than the one you are already working on. If not, add them to your list in order of priority.

4. When you have completed the first five jobs as far as you can, make another list of the next five jobs. It's not a problem if you can't do everything on the list – at least the most important jobs will be completed.

Schwab agreed to ask his managers to put this advice into practice for a month and then pay Lee whatever he felt it was worth. A month later, he sent Lee a cheque for $25,000, equivalent to almost $300,000 in today's money. Schwab later said that it was the single most useful piece of information he had ever received and he believed it was immensely significant in the success of the company.

Give it a try and you will find it does work beautifully. You have to be very disciplined if the top things on your list are tasks you hate doing, but I guarantee it does pay off if you 'eat the frog'.

> **Just a thought:**
> Don't worry if you can't seem to churn out work at a consistent rate. I find a 'good' productive day is usually followed by a day of doing 'bitty' things, but it's all necessary to the process. Without that bitty day you wouldn't have the resources for the productive one.

Avoiding time wasters

Beware of what Americans call 'busy work', jobs that make you feel as though you are making progress towards getting your work done but which are not really achieving anything. They can easily become pure procrastination. And there are some jobs which will happily swallow up all the time you can give them but yield very few results. These are the ones to watch out for.

DEALING WITH EMAILS

Making some simple rules about how you use and process emails will save you time. Here are my favourite email tips:

☐ Only download your emails two or three times a day – mid-morning and mid-afternoon would be good times, as it gives people time to send stuff to you in the morning, and in the afternoon you will have time to respond before the end of the day. Reply straightaway. It's easy to think 'I'll deal with that later' and then forget.

☐ Immediately delete as many emails as possible, or move them into named folders for later use. Your inbox will then only contain emails requiring action or those awaiting a reply. Out of sight can all too easily be out of mind if you need to scroll down to see emails in your inbox.

☐ Be specific when writing subject headings and try to use information which will easily identify the email, such as names, dates and times. Sometimes you will need to find a particular email again quickly, and unique subject headings will avoid that time-consuming trawl through a long list, all with subjects like 'Invoice' or 'Meeting'.

☐ Draft standard responses to regular enquiries and keep the templates in your Draft folder, but be sure you personalise every detail before sending them out. If you have taken time and care to write a friendly message, you don't want to ruin its effect by alerting the reader to the fact it's a standard draft.

☐ Emails may be great for keeping in touch, but sometimes phone calls are still the faster and easier option, for example if you need to contact a group of people to change arrangements. You can never assume an email has reached its destination, or that the response to it hasn't gone astray.

☐ It can be tempting to use email to avoid talking to someone, particularly if there is a problem to resolve, but this is the very time you do need to speak to them. The tone and intention of emails can be easily misunderstood, and the situation might just escalate.

☐ Always re-read emails before pressing the Send key to pick up typing errors and check for possible misinterpretation. You know what was in your mind when you typed it, but the reader might understand something else entirely. If the matter is important, try to leave enough time to draft an email and go back to it after a while. With fresh eyes you may see some changes to make.

☐ I hesitate to mention this last point as it seems so obvious, but I still come across it from time to time – EMAILS TYPED IN CAPITALS. Presumably the sender feels the contents are important but it only comes across as hectoring and creates a bad impression.

CONDUCTING MEETINGS

No longer having to attend the frequent meetings imposed on you at work is undoubtedly one of the advantages of working from home, but sometimes a face-to-face meeting is still the best way of communicating.

A very successful businessman once told me his secret for effective meetings – don't let anyone sit down! I assume he was joking, however much he might have wanted to do it, so short of taking the chairs out of the room, what can you do to expedite proceedings? These guidelines have worked well for me:

☐ If possible, avoid late afternoon and just after lunch, as these are the worst times for concentration.

☐ Circulate an agenda to everyone at least a day before so they can come prepared. Also agree beforehand who will be the chairman (someone who is tactful but firm and can stop people going off at a tangent) and who will take and write up the minutes (someone who can grasp the key points and write them up concisely).

☐ Have a finishing time as well as a start time. Start the meeting punctually, check the clock periodically to keep on track and finish on time. Don't interrupt proceedings to recap for latecomers or you will end up overrunning.

☐ Summarise action points at the end to make sure everyone knows what they need to achieve.

☐ Do you ever get invited to meetings and wonder why your presence is required? If you have nothing to contribute, and nothing to learn, don't feel obliged to attend; make your excuses and ask for the minutes to be sent to you afterwards.

USING THE PHONE

Talking on the phone can be a real time-waster. My personal pet hate is people who ramble on and on, repeating themselves and not taking their cue when you attempt you wind up the conversation. You can't do much about them, but you can watch your own telephone use. These are my rules to stop calls eating up my day.

☐ Only switch on your mobile when you want to use it. I am completely opposed to the expectation that we should all be available 24 hours a day. I find it intrusive and unnecessary. As far as I am concerned, my mobile phone is for my convenience and no-one else's.

☐ Don't hesitate to put on the answerphone if you want to concentrate on a piece of work (or have a nap!) Nobody expects you to be instantly available all day, every day, and people are accustomed to leaving a message. Just make sure you listen to your messages at the earliest opportunity and remember to ring back quickly.

☐ Make sure you have all the information to hand *before* you dial the number. It's exasperating for the person you're talking to, and embarrassing for you, if you don't have obvious details like account numbers when you make a call. Similarly, try to keep paper and a pen by the phone – it's always the person you want to impress who catches you without them.

☐ Are you in the right frame of mind to make this particular call? Your mood is conveyed by your tone of voice and will be picked up by the person you speak to. If you are feeling out of sorts, or have to make a sales call and don't feel up to it, then it might be better to wait until you are feeling more positive. But don't let it turn into procrastination. If you find making calls hard, practice will improve them.

☐ Watch out for spending time chatting after you have resolved your business query. Time can just disappear by doing this.

CONTROLLING PAPER

When I was at school in the 1970s, I remember being shown a film about the office of the future, the 'paperless office'. There was also a film about the huge amount of leisure time we would all be enjoying, thanks to the growing wonders of technology. As with so many predictions about the future, these two have proved to be ill-founded, and paper rolls into our lives in an unstoppable and ever-increasing flow. It threatens to swamp us if we do not deal with it promptly. Here's how to deal with it.

☐ Deal with post as soon as it arrives. Much can be dumped or recycled immediately, but in these days of identity theft, remember to shred anything that reveals personal information. Be ruthless. If you are tempted to keep something to 'read later', be aware that it will probably never get read, just accumulate on your desk in a growing, depressing pile. Information is now so readily available, and changes so frequently, that articles date very quickly and if you do need that information in the future you will probably have to check the facts again anyway.

☐ If you really think you may want to refer to a piece of paper in the future, file it away, but make a diary note to clear files at least once a year – the end of the tax year is a good time, as once six years are up you will be able to ditch a year's tax and business records. Every time I have my annual session on the shredder I am amazed by how much stuff I've carefully kept and then completely forgotten about.

☐ If you find you are constantly picking things up and putting them down to 'sort out later', get out a red pen. Each time you look at the page, put a red dot in the corner. With any luck, the proliferation of red dots will encourage you to deal with it and get it out of the way!

Procrastination and what you can do about it

This is the big one for homeworkers, isn't it? I think we all procrastinate to some extent. You put off something which you know you've got to do at some point, and which actually you could do straightaway. You put it off to try and make life more pleasant, but often end up making yourself feel stressed and guilty instead. There are many ways you can procrastinate and some of them masquerade as being helpful. See if you recognise any of these.

☐ You carry on researching and gathering material long after you should have started on the task. You tell yourself this is vital background information but in fact you are just putting off the evil moment.

☐ You start to obsessively clean and tidy your immediate environment, well beyond necessity's sake. You can't start that job until you have absolutely the right equipment, furniture, computer, reference materials etc.

☐ Suddenly all sorts of other jobs take priority – the kitchen floor has to be washed, the oven cleaned, the ironing done. It's all useful activity but underneath you know very well it's not getting you any closer to achieving that dreaded task.

SO WHY DO WE PROCRASTINATE?

There are many reasons for putting things off. In the simplest instances, it's because you find the job boring or perhaps you don't quite understand what is required. If that is the case, there are simple practical steps you can take to rectify the situation – get somebody else to do it, for example! Particularly when you are running your own business, it really does pay to concentrate on your strengths, which bring in the money, and pay someone else to do the bits you hate and never get around to. Doing the books is a prime example, and you can also get other people to deal with correspondence, chase payment of invoices and make sales calls.

Sometimes there are more insidious reasons which stop your progress and it might help to think whether any of these are applicable. Just identifying them can help you to start overcoming them.

☐ Maybe you're feeling overwhelmed by the sheer quantity of work you have to do, and the worry makes you unable to focus on making a start.

☐ You might be afraid of failing – 'I've never been any good at this sort of thing. What if I make a mess of it and show myself up?' Or you may actually fear success – 'What will happen if I do really well in this? Will people still like me? What else might I have to do?'

☐ You suffer from perfectionism or unrealistically high standards. You might want to read everything you can find on a subject before starting to write it up, and keep finding new material.

☐ You might be expecting your first attempts to resemble the finished product, and get put off when your efforts look amateur or inadequate.

TACKLING PROCRASTINATION

Don't wait until the situation is desperate and you've made yourself miserable before you get started. The following suggestions should help you to deal with any of the above reasons for putting something off.

☐ You know that horrible sinking feeling when despite yourself the thought of that long-postponed task slips into your mind? Sometimes actually getting down to it can come as a relief. Try turning it round in your mind – 'Today I *will* do that thing and it will be a pleasure because then I won't have it at the back of my mind any more.'

☐ As long as cleaning and tidying your office isn't one of your ways of procrastinating, having a good old clear up can be a way of kick-starting the brain. Making space in your physical environment can somehow make a space in your mind for new ideas to flow into.

☐ Remember that the most difficult moment is the first moment. If you can just get started, you begin to build up momentum and the further you go, the greater the momentum, until you are carried along almost without volition.

☐ Break the job into a number of small, easily-achievable chunks. Do the first and then reward yourself by making a coffee or having a look at the paper. Continue like this in short bursts and you might find the magical momentum building up.

☐ Or you could start with the job you find easiest or like the best. Maybe it's not the logical place to start, but if it gets you fired up, you can slot it into place later.

☐ A report or piece of written work can be hard to make a start on, as you already have the finished piece in your mind's eye, and it's difficult to know where to start. Have a brainstorm and write down all the ideas you associate with the subject. Group together the points into categories and you will begin to see how to develop your argument. The hard work is done; now you can concentrate on expressing your ideas.

☐ If you're feeling overwhelmed, then follow the advice of Ivy Lee from the 1930s (Making the most of your time, page 88). Take a deep breath, sit down with a piece of paper and list all your jobs in order of priority. Start with the most important and work on it until it's finished or you've done as much as you can. Then go on to the second most important job etc.

Just a thought:
Putting something off for a while may not always be a bad thing – sometimes if you start by making notes and then leave them for a while, your subconscious comes up with creative ideas you would never have thought of if you had conscientiously kept on working.

Resources

☐ The kettle – taking frequent breaks will stop your brain getting too tired and maintain your productivity.

☐ *Clear Your Clutter with Feng Shui* by Karen Kingston. Piatkus, 1998.
Down-to-earth advice on getting rid of accumulated 'stuff' and becoming more effective.

☐ www.productivity501.com
A site full of articles and tips on how to increase your personal productivity.

☐ www.hassleme.co.uk
Keep forgetting to do the things you know you should? You can ask hassleme.com to email you at the intervals you choose to remind you to get those important tasks done.

☐ *The War of Art: Break Through the Blocks and Win Your Inner Creative Battles* by Steven Pressfield. Grand Central Publishing, 2003.
Read this book and stop putting off the things you really want to do but never seem to get round to. Pressfield is a bestselling novelist who understands the subject of resistance inside out and will inspire you to get moving with your

most cherished dreams. You can sample an excerpt at
www.stevenpressfield.com/books/war_art.asp#excerpt

☐ www.mozarteffect.com
Scientists have discovered that different types of music activate different parts of
the brain. Research has been carried out into the music of Mozart, which has
been found to be beneficial to learning and health. The FAQs on this site give
more information about this collection of CDs and the 'Focus and Clarity' set is
reputed to aid concentration and alertness while reading and studying.

☐ www.tpsonline.org.uk/tps
The Telephone Preference Service is a free service where you can register your
preference not to receive unsolicited sales and marketing phone calls to your
home and mobile numbers. There is also a Corporate TPS.
At the same site you can find out about the Mail Preference Service which cuts
off all that unwanted direct mail.

SOME SUGGESTIONS FOR SITES TO BROWSE AS YOU GENTLY TUNE IN TO WORK

☐ www.guardian.co.uk

☐ www.independent.co.uk

☐ www.telegraph.co.uk

☐ www.timesonline.co.uk
Keep up with the latest news.

☐ www.metoffice.org.uk
Plan your day around the weather by checking the forecast for your local area.

☐ www.veryshortlist.com
Receive an email every weekday recommending quirky books, films, music,
websites, and the latest arty adverts.

☐ www.enterprisequest.com
Sign up for a free weekly bulletin of tips and ideas for home business owners.

☐ www.thesartorialist.blogspot.com
A fascinating glimpse of people and fashion in New York and other stylish
capitals around the world.

6
WHAT ABOUT MY PROFESSIONAL IMAGE?

You may spend a lot of time working at home and invisible to the rest of the world, but it's still essential to look professional and behave in a professional manner.

This chapter covers three areas crucial to all homeworkers whether you are employed or working for yourself, followed by sections tailored firstly to the needs of those in employment and then those who are running home businesses:

1. The need to maintain confidentiality in conversation and written material in the relaxed environment of your own home.

2. Ways to consistently provide such outstanding customer service (bearing in mind you may be 'serving' colleagues rather than paying customers) that you will always be in demand.

3. How to present yourself in everything you do so that people believe in you and trust you to be businesslike.

4. Tips for employed homeworkers on keeping up with the game even though you don't see your colleagues on a daily basis.

5. Tips for the self-employed on conveying a coherent brand to everyone you deal with.

The importance of confidentiality

Working in the privacy of your own home, away from the eyes of colleagues and visitors, it can be easy to slip into an over-relaxed attitude about the confidentiality of the information you're dealing with. I'm not suggesting that your family or visiting friends might use the information for unscrupulous ends, but you owe your clients and colleagues a high level of vigilance. Failure to observe this could result in the loss of work or your reputation, and that is hard to recover from. Maintain high levels of confidentiality in the following ways.

☐ Have your own separate space for you to have somewhere to read documents and make phone calls without being overlooked or overheard. This is a great help.

☐ Make sure you lock documents away in a filing cabinet when you have finished using them and keep computer passwords away from other family members. (See Chapter 8 for a sobering story on what could happen if you don't.)

Just a thought:
Choose a shredder that is up to the job — you can get them for home, office and heavy-duty use, and the type designed for home use may not be adequate if you use it often. Strip-cut shredders cut the paper into thin strips, while cross-cut shredders cut it into small pieces and are therefore more suitable for confidential information.

☐ If you are self-employed, find out if you should register as a data gatherer under the Data Protection Act. Surprisingly few businesses are exempt.

☐ Make arrangements for daily data back-up, off-site if necessary. Losing confidential information is as bad as disclosing it to the wrong people.

☐ Be careful when using your mobile phone in a public place; you never know who might be able to hear you.

☐ Avoid a careless reference to your work or the people you deal with in conversations with friends. It's all too easy to inadvertently mention a name when your business and your casual chats are conducted in the same space, possibly even on the same phone. 'So-and-so told me the other day . . . ' can slip out before you know it, so if in doubt, don't mention that topic or get into the habit of always adhering to the Chatham House Rule.

THE CHATHAM HOUSE RULE

Chatham House is the home of the Royal Institute of International Affairs and the Rule was created almost a hundred years ago to promote freedom of discussion on sensitive topics. The Rule says 'When a meeting, or part thereof, is held under the Chatham House Rule, participants are free to use the information received, but neither the identity nor the affiliation of the speaker(s), nor that of any other participant, may be revealed.'

In other words you may disclose a particular piece of information but not who gave it to you or the name of the organisation they belong to.

Providing excellent customer service

We all have customers, although the people you work for may not pay you directly for the work you do for them. If you work in the public sector your customers might be the people who live in your local authority area while your work is funded by government taxes. Or your customers could be your colleagues in the same or another department, who rely on your efforts to support them to deliver a service.

It's said that 70% of dissatisfied customers take their business elsewhere, not for reasons of price or finding a better product, but because they are unhappy with the level of personal attention they are receiving. If you get your customer service right you have a much higher chance of hanging on to your current customers and not having to spend the time and money to find new ones.

Customer service is a huge subject and there are hundreds of books on it and millions of pages on the internet. It's not my intention to give you exhaustive coverage of the subject here, just to provide some points I've found particularly pertinent while working from home and running a small business.

GIVE A CONSISTENTLY GOOD EXPERIENCE

It's important your customers can rely on getting a good experience each and every time they deal with you. If the quality is variable they will gradually stop coming back, even if they like you.

A Story of Occasional Brilliance

' *When we lived in West Cornwall, we went to try out a much reviewed restaurant. We had a lovely evening and enjoyed delicious, well cooked food served by friendly and efficient staff, so we returned on another occasion. But then we took a friend who had to send his lamb back, twice. And another time we arrived to find they had unilaterally decided to seat us at a table in the garden, just as the sun was going down and it was getting chilly. So we stopped going because we couldn't rely on it being a consistently good experience and we didn't feel like taking the chance. Occasional brilliance doesn't cut it.* '

STAND OUT IN THE MARKETPLACE

How many businesses do you deal with, on either a personal or work basis, that stand out from the crowd? Not many, I'll bet. And what's your reaction when you do come across one of these gems? You can't stop talking about it, telling people how amazing it is, and you go out of your way to use it as often as possible. You can probably achieve a level of success by being mediocre, but where's the fun in that? Why be indistinguishable from the crowd when with a little extra effort you can stand out?

The fact is that you don't actually have to do a lot to be special. To quote Woody Allen, '80% of success is showing up' and in some trades that is enough to put you head and shoulders above the competition. Emma's husband is a plumber and sometimes she gets phone calls from customers after he has called on them: 'People are quite surprised when my husband turns up when we say he will. They say "Your husband's just been" and I say "Yes, that's right, you were booked in for today" and they're just amazed.'

UNDER-PROMISE AND OVER-DELIVER

The importance of this was brought home to me when I bought a book from Amazon. They give you an estimated delivery date and so you mentally prepare to wait until then – but then the book turned up several days before. Result – one delighted customer. This is so easy to do that it's hard to believe that so many businesses get it wrong. If your customer wants something and you know it will take a while, resist the impulse to initially please them by giving an over-optimistic completion date. Make sure you over-estimate the time instead, so that when you deliver 'early' the customer is thrilled and amazed by your efficiency.

DO WHAT YOU CLAIM TO DO

What is important is the customer's perception of you, and they will judge you on what you do, not what you say. You may espouse certain values and beliefs and yet fail to convey them to your customer or to act in accordance with them. What you think about your service and the way you deliver it is irrelevant – it is the feeling you create when your customer deals with you that matters. If they are left with a negative feeling it is unlikely they will return.

You Do What?

We recently went to a newly opened café where the menus proudly displayed the values of the proprietors, including their commitment to providing a welcoming environment and good service. All very well and good, but unfortunately the young staff appeared to be quite unaware of these claims or at least unable to deliver on them – as we found a table, looked at the menu and waited to order, they did that 'I can't see you' thing that many shop assistants have down to a fine art. In the end I went up to the counter and was met with a blank stare. The food was OK but we left feeling unwelcome and uncared-for and I doubt we'll return.

DEAL WITH COMPLAINTS

We are only human, and from time to time errors and oversights inevitably occur, so don't be horrified if you get a complaint. What counts is how you respond, not the fact there has been a complaint. In fact a complaint is an opportunity to strengthen your relationship with that person or organisation, just as you may have noticed that conflict, as long as it is followed by resolution, makes you closer to your friends.

Occasionally when I was running my cleaning business, I'd get a call from a client complaining that a bin hadn't been emptied the previous evening. Hardly a life-or-death situation and one which could be rectified at the next clean, but I always made a point of driving round to the office as soon as possible and emptying it myself, to show my clients that their needs were important to me and I would act promptly on their requests.

Not all complaints are so easily rectified and sometimes the event that gave rise to it has already occurred and cannot be changed. In that case, ask the client 'What can I do to make it up to you?' or 'How can I restore your faith in me?' They might come up with something quite surprising but do whatever they suggest (within reason, of course). They will be so delighted at your response that the complaint will be forgotten.

> **Just a thought:**
> It always pays to stay on good terms with everyone you meet in the course of your work, no matter how trying you find them. You just never know where they will pop up next.

KEEP COMMUNICATING

You know how unnerving it is when you order something or ask for a service and then you don't hear anything from the shop or tradesman? After a while you start to doubt what was agreed, and wonder whether they've forgotten or maybe didn't want the business in the first place. I always feel slightly aggrieved if I have to do the chasing. After all, I'm the customer, shouldn't they be chasing my business? Keep in contact with your customers in these ways.

- ☐ Make courtesy calls to confirm upcoming appointments or just to tell them there is no news yet, but you're keeping on top of it.

- ☐ Keep your customer updated if the agreed schedule slips. I'm not suggesting you shouldn't make every effort to meet a deadline, but if you are struggling to finish on time a quick phone call might get you an extension.

- ☐ Check your messages frequently and get back to callers without delay.

- ☐ Don't forget the old-fashioned methods of communication – sometimes it's quicker and simpler to ring instead of emailing, and snail mail still has its uses.

- ☐ Make sure you can be contacted easily. Put all contact details (phone numbers, fax number, business address, email address and website URL) on all your stationery and as a signature on your emails.

- ☐ Always answer your phone with at least your name, and perhaps your company name as well, never just 'Hello'. It sounds completely unprofessional and starts business calls off on the wrong foot.

- ☐ Be very wary of letting young children answer the phone. Some people may be charmed, but for others it is a real turn-off.

A Plumber's Story

Emma runs the admin. side of her husband's plumbing business: 'I have trained my daughters not to answer the phone and to be quiet when I am making calls to customers and they are very respectful of that. When they have friends round I hear them say "We've got to be very quiet now, because Mummy's on the phone."'

Train older children to answer the phone as you would, and to take a message. If your children hog the phone it might be time to get a separate business line installed.

- ☐ Record messages on your mobile and telephone so people know they've reached the right number, and update them to reflect your current circumstances – 'I'll be in conference until Thursday 20th but I'll be checking messages and will get back to you as soon as I can.'

- ☐ Also see Chapter 5 for hints on controlling the amount of time you spend on the phone and dealing expeditiously with emails.

- ☐ Don't pass on chain emails or jokes to business contacts or customers; they are unlikely to thank you. Also beware of emails asking for support for political causes, warning of viruses and asking for help in tracing missing people – although it beggars belief, a huge proportion are spoofs.

Looking and acting the part

You're working at home and nobody's going to see what you're wearing so it doesn't matter what you throw on, does it? Actually clothes do have a huge effect on mood and confidence, and their impact on productivity is discussed in Chapter 5, but in this section we're concerned with those times when people are going to see you, either in your home office or out in the big, wide world.

Numerous studies have shown that we make judgements about new people on the basis of the first few minutes of meeting them, and that those first impressions are extremely hard to change later. It's therefore crucial that your appearance and behaviour project the right image to your clients, associates and the general public. The right image certainly starts with what you wear and how well groomed you are, but it embraces a lot more too.

THE RIGHT CLOTHES

I know it's glaringly obvious but always wear the kind of clothes appropriate to your occupation. It's not just a question of cleanliness and condition – turning up in unsuitable clothes will put people off their stroke and make them question your suitability for the job.

When Jeans are Business Clothes

My clients were all professional people with their own image to keep up. They used me and not one of my many competitors because they could trust me to make sure the cleaning always got done, and their clients would not be turning up in the morning to a dirty office. I therefore always wore clean jeans, T shirt and jacket or cardigan to visit existing and prospective clients, to convey the message that I was a hands-on boss who would roll my sleeves up if necessary to get the job done. I remember once going to give a quote for an office cleaning contract and bumping into a competitor who was just leaving. He was wearing a natty navy blazer, shirt, tie and slacks. Perfectly suitable for a business appointment, but strongly suggesting that he would manage from a distance and not get involved with the nitty-gritty of cleaning. That would have been perfectly acceptable to some clients, but they were not my market.

If you're not sure about what to wear or what suits you, ask someone who is always well turned-out for their advice. If you're not sure about asking friends for help – and the danger is that you end up as their clone – many department stores offer a free personal shopper who will handpick a selection from across the store for you to try. They should give objective feedback rather than subjecting you to the hard sell, but there is usually no obligation to buy. The friend might come in useful if you feel you need moral support or a second opinion.

Getting your colours done by a professional consultant might seem expensive but I've never come across anyone who regretted the investment. Wearing the colours that suit and uplift you makes a huge difference to your appearance and confidence, whether you are male or female. Ask if the consultation will also cover the style of clothes that best suit your body shape, for example, tailored or more flowing. Once you know that you will wonder how you made mistakes so often before and you'll save lots of money by not buying anything that doesn't flatter you.

Just a thought:
'You have a much better life if you wear impressive clothes.'
Vivienne Westwood, fashion designer

PERSONAL HYGIENE

It might seem superfluous to mention personal hygiene now there are so many grooming products for both men and women, but the fact is I do still encounter people in work situations with BO, bad breath and dirty hair. That kind of person is so unaware that they are unlikely to be reading this book, but maybe if you know one, you'd like to pass it on to them with a bookmark in this page. Seriously though, stressful situations like interviews and tricky meetings can literally make us sweat, as can public transport in the summer, so be prepared and don't be the subject of office gossip. Many years ago, while working as a personnel officer, I had to give the 'I'm afraid you smell' talk to a member of staff and it was very uncomfortable.

BAD HABITS

I used to know someone who ran his own business and was popular with everyone who knew him – but I can't have been the only person to notice his habit of constantly scratching his groin. We all tend to have unconscious habits that surface when we're nervous, and that we're totally unaware of until someone points them out or until we get videoed at work. Most aren't quite as extreme as my example, but repeated nose scratching, hair pulling or playing with jewellery can be irritating and undermine your professional image. Plus, if the last two are done by women, they can give a business encounter a flirtatious edge that might be very unwelcome.

ACCESSORIES AND EQUIPMENT

Anything you wear or carry with you is as much a statement about you as your clothes, so think about the little details too. Here is my list of fashion clangers.

- ☐ Don't neglect your shoes. You may not be looking at them much but other people are. Keep them well polished and in good repair. They'll last longer if you don't wear the same pair two days in a row.

- ☐ Don't wear more than a minimum of jewellery (whether you're male or female). A little too much jewellery on men can easily give off a Del-boy image. A classy watch, cufflinks and wedding ring are enough. Women don't enhance their business image with clattering bracelets that constantly need pushing back, fingers loaded with rings and an armoury of necklaces. That said, it is supposed to be helpful for women's confidence to wear a necklace or a scarf; something to do with covering the throat, a vulnerable part of the body. In my business adviser days I had a favourite pair of large silver earrings in a shield design that I always wore if I expected a difficult day, as I felt armed for battle when I put them on.

- ☐ Don't show cleavage, ladies, much less a flash of bra. Exposing flesh has become much more acceptable in the last decade or so, but I'd always save it for your free time. Do you really want your business colleagues staring down your shirt as you discuss sales figures? Skirt lengths tell their own stories as well – too short and you risk looking tarty, too long and you are entering hippy-dippy territory. Perhaps that's why so many working women play it safe and stick to trousers.

☐ Don't wear 'jokey' socks or ties, chaps, the kind with cartoon characters and lurid colours. In some quarters they are claimed to show what a wag you are; to most people they just look really sad.

☐ Don't forget your briefcase/laptop/mobile/handbag – all affect your image so choose them accordingly and keep them in good shape. While in the cleaning industry I once bought, and then quickly stopped using, a stylish leather briefcase because I felt it gave the impression I was office-bound, quite the opposite of the way I ran my business. Instead I went back to a colourful African basket that held everything I needed, including spare cleaning supplies.

CARS

Whether you have a company car or drive your own, you never know when you might be asked to give a lift to the managing director or an important client, so clean it regularly inside and out. People with dogs or small children are at a disadvantage here, I'm afraid, and there's no getting away from the fact that smokers' cars smell horrible to non-smokers.

When I became a business adviser I was still driving the old Renault 5 that had been adequate as a runaround for the cleaning business, but now didn't exactly put across the message I needed of a successful businesswoman able to advise others. Until I was able to replace it with a newer car there were several occasions when I was forced to park some distance away from a venue and walk the rest of the way, so as not to detract from my new besuited image.

ETIQUETTE

Etiquette sounds such a dated word, but it simply means having consideration for other people and being able to put them at ease in business or social situations. If you can do that, your professional reputation will benefit.

Timekeeping

Chapter 2 examines possible reasons why some people always manage to be on time while others are chronically late. If you're one of the unfortunates who find it difficult to be on time, you'll end up working hard to win back all the brownie points you've lost to irritated colleagues if you don't give yourself enough reminders such as setting the alarm on your mobile.

Business meals

Going out for business meals with people you don't know very well can be an intimidating experience, but these guidelines might help you to relax, make a good impression and even enjoy yourself.

- ☐ Switch off your mobile as you approach the restaurant, as it's easy to forget once the greetings and introductions start.

- ☐ As a general rule, the person who suggested the meeting pays for the meal. If you meet again, then take your turn to foot the bill. If you're not sure how the bill will be split, ask when you arrive. Leaving it till later might make you anxious and lead to one of those embarrassing 'No, please, I insist' conversations.

- ☐ If someone else is paying, don't order the most expensive dishes on the menu; pick something at a mid-range price. This is not the best time to order messy food (hold the spaghetti bolognese) or complicated dishes that you are not familiar with.

- ☐ Let your host lead the small talk and don't leap into business matters until he brings up the subject.

- ☐ Many business meals are conducted with no alcohol and you will feel awkward if you are the only one who indulges, so follow the lead of your host. The same applies to dessert. If there is alcohol, drink moderately.

- ☐ If you are not happy with your food and don't know your host well, you may choose to overlook the fault for the sake of developing a good relationship. If there is a serious problem or you already know your host quite well, make them aware of your concern and let them take it up with the waiter.

- ☐ As in any other form of networking, follow up the meal with a thank you email, call or note and take whatever actions you agreed to over the meal.

- ☐ If you are making the arrangements, establish from your guests how much time they've got and choose the venue accordingly, preferably somewhere you know and can trust to provide a good experience. Some restaurants offer quick service at lunchtime for business customers. You might want to avoid peak times or very noisy places.

- ☐ For an important meeting, go somewhere you have already built a good relationship with the staff. Speak to the head waiter or manager in advance if you have a special request, such as a table in a quiet corner where you can't be overheard.

☐ Tip well if you have been served well and you will continue to receive good treatment that will impress your guests.

Just a thought:

'Manners are a sensitive awareness of the feelings of others. If you have that awareness, you have good manners, no matter what fork you use'.

Emily Post, American writer on etiquette

Entertaining

Every Christmas, newspapers and magazines produce the usual articles on how to behave at the office party – don't get blind drunk, photocopy your bottom, try to kiss the temp etc. We all know the rules by now (although knowing them doesn't mean that we keep them). But what about social gatherings organised by business associates or networking groups when the rules don't seem quite so necessary? Can you kick back and relax, or is there still a need for a little propriety? I was once invited to a party held by someone I'd met in a business context who also invited lots of other business contacts. He spent the evening getting extremely drunk and trying to persuade his guests to drink massive quantities of alcohol too. I couldn't keep that school-boyish behaviour from tarnishing my impression of him in his work role. Keep drunken evenings for close family and friends, the people who are most likely to forgive bad behaviour.

Say thank you

Saying thank you is one of the most powerful ways to make a good impression and is all too easily overlooked. In the headlong rush to get things done, we tend to take for granted the things that go well and only get excited about the problems and glitches. I learnt this over and over again in the cleaning business, where we could clean an office for months and never hear a word, but I'd get a phone call of complaint if a small detail was overlooked on one occasion. I used to tell my cleaners that 'No news is good news in this business' but naturally they became demoralised if they got no recognition from our clients.

People love to be thanked for what they do, out of all proportion to the amount of time and effort it takes to pick up the phone, fire off an email or write a card. (Chapter 2 provides information on how to show appreciation in the best way for each individual.) And on a purely selfish level, showing appreciation for someone is the best way to make sure they keep delivering the goods. I know that whenever someone has thanked me for my efforts, it has made me determined to never let them down in the future.

DEALING WITH PEOPLE ABROAD

The world has shrunk due to the power and reach of the internet and modern communications and it's now quite common for even small businesses to deal with people all over the world. From time to time you might be required to meet them in person and it's vital you realise that the customs and values we take for granted here may be quite different in other societies. Much more emphasis may be placed on hierarchy, qualifications or family in other parts of the world, so do your research before you depart on your trip to avoid making a faux pas and not even realising you've done it.

The Never-Ending Stream of Business Cards

❝ *This may well be an urban myth, but I once heard a story about a hapless British businessman who visited Japan without troubling to find out that the giving and receiving of business cards, far from the casual matter it is here, is treated there as a little ceremony. Cards are offered and taken with both hands, studied intently, commented respectfully upon and kept on the table during the meeting. This individual casually took a card and stuffed it in his back pocket, whereupon his Japanese associate offered him another, which he took and stuffed into his back pocket, and so on.....* ❞

PLANNING

Know your stuff

The old Boy Scout adage 'Be prepared' applies equally well to the homeworker. Just because you work at home doesn't mean you shouldn't know all about your own company, its competitors, trading partners, developments in the industry and possible future trends. You never know who you might meet and want to impress at a networking meeting or even at the school gates.

Keep stock

As well as being on the ball with regard to relevant information, it's a good idea to always have stocks of your tools of the trade, so you can cope with a sudden rush or something breaking down. Keep a back-up supply of stationery and stock and see Chapter 9 for contingency planning for a crisis.

Keeping up with the game when you're employed

There is a danger that working from home may not enhance your career or your chances of promotion, either because company culture regards it as showing less commitment ('something women do after they've had children') or because you are less visible to your bosses. It's essential that you keep on top of office news and developments while working from home, for the sake of your peace of mind as well as your career development.

☐ There's always somebody in any office who can be guaranteed to know what's going on. Identify that person, whoever they are – it could be the receptionist or somebody you don't work with directly – and keep in regular touch with them. Let them know you appreciate them by finding out how they like to be thanked (see Chapter 2).

☐ Encourage your colleagues to keep in touch by contacting them regularly by phone and email. Sarah is a sales executive whose head office is hundreds of miles away from her home: 'You have to go the extra mile because you're not in the office. I phone people regularly for a chat – it's our version of going to make a coffee.'

☐ If you are within striking distance of the office, attend all the meetings and training sessions organised for your team, for the personal contact as well as making others aware that you are still an active member of the team.

☐ Similarly, go along to all the social events, the evenings out, birthday celebrations, Christmas dinners and industry occasions.

☐ Whatever you choose to wear in the privacy of your workspace, take care to maintain the required corporate image when you visit the office or go out to see clients. Some dress codes are quite rigid. A senior manager of a blue chip company I know of had a reputation for marching his sales staff to Marks and Spencers to buy a plain, dark suit and white shirts if they showed up in anything else. There was method in his madness – in his best-selling book about small business *The E Myth Revisited*, Michael Gerber reveals that people are more likely to buy from someone wearing these clothes and colours than they are from someone wearing brown, no matter how well-presented.

You need to devise ways of communicating well with your boss and in particular letting them know about your successes and high level of productivity.

☐ Get to know their interests to help you anticipate their moods and the best time to approach them. A rabid football supporter is likely to be disgruntled the morning after his team suffer a resounding defeat.

☐ Regard your manager as you would a customer and anticipate their needs so that you have done something before they ask for it.

☐ Your job is to help your manager look good, so find out how you can help them most, with their personal as well as their professional objectives. The more you help them, the more they will help you.

☐ Give them success stories to feed their bosses – if you look good, they look good too.

☐ Don't withhold bad news but think about possible solutions before you break it to them.

☐ Take the time to understand how they like to communicate (see Chapter 2). Do they prefer to talk or receive information by email? Do they like to meet for coffee or lunch? How much detail do they need?

Consistent branding for the self-employed

I read somewhere that it takes seven 'touches' – mentions or sights of your business – before the buying public absorb something about who you are and what you do. It's vital that those seven touches all communicate the same message or you may never get through to your market. You can communicate in many ways, such as the vehicle you drive, ads in places as varied as the local paper or the back of a bus, your staff uniform, website, business cards and correspondence, signs displayed at the premises you are working on, and so on.

Your branding or identity, no matter how small your business, should be carefully chosen to convey what you do and how you do business. You can express all this and more by clever choice of colours, lettering and logo. A professional designer will understand how people perceive colour and design, what is memorable and the factors most likely to inspire people to buy, and so they are worth consulting if you can afford to. If funds are very limited, a simple design need not cost a lot.

A Roofer's Story

When Vince started his business he designed a logo himself, which is featured on his van, headed paper and compliment slips, scaffold banners and the polo shirts he and his employee wear. His wife, Claire, runs the paperwork side of the business and her aim is to provide a professional service from the moment people phone asking for a quote, through the correspondence that goes out giving prices and the calls she makes to customers to keep them informed of progress and if necessary reschedule jobs.

Having decided on a suitable identity, the work is not over, as anything carrying your logo must be clean and well presented. I mentioned in Chapter 3 that my own cleaning business grew out of an attempt to spruce up the traditional image of a window cleaner. Emma and her husband run a plumbing business and 'are very aware of the image of a plumber as a bloke in a flat cap driving a clapped out car. We want to portray something quite different.' To that end they clean the van every week and Emma makes sure all the estimates, letters and invoices she sends out are properly spelt and well written.

With a good corporate image you can punch above your weight – nobody has to know you are a small business based at home. Emma again: 'Sometimes people ring up and ask if 'someone' can come out to them, as though we have a team of plumbers. I don't say "Oh, it's just my husband." I say "My husband will come and see you" and then they think they're getting the boss.'

A Moveable Ad

❝ Our logo was professionally designed and painted on the side of a Suzuki jeep, a fashionable vehicle in the 1980s. We parked it in the centre of Bath several times a day while we were cleaning offices and it generated a lot of business as people noticed it and rang to enquire about our services. Twice we were approached by people visiting Bath who wanted to know if we were a franchise that would sell them a licence to trade in their home town. ❞

It's not just a case of making sure that the physical items representing your business have the right image. The people you associate with are even more likely to tarnish or enhance your reputation.

HOW STAFF AFFECT YOUR PROFESSIONAL IMAGE

The legalities and bureaucracy involved in employing staff are covered in Chapter 3 but the human side of recruiting, training and supervising employees is an important consideration on its own. The public and your customers do not make a distinction between you, your business and your staff. To the world at large, your staff *are* your business, and they have the capacity to cover you with glory or lose your reputation with a misplaced remark. Finding and keeping great staff is by no means easy and the shortage of good part-time cleaners was the main reason I sold my business. Many small businesses have expanded to take on staff, only to shrink again when the responsibilities became too onerous. You'll get off to the best start by following these guidelines.

☐ Be selective. Employing the friend of someone you know does sometimes work, but often you find yourself accommodating *their* preferences for hours and duties. Start by getting clear in your own mind what you need an employee to do, how they should do it, when, where and for how much pay. Advertise the vacancy where you think that person has the best chance of seeing it. It could be in the window of the corner shop, at the Jobcentre, in the local paper, or all three.

☐ When people respond, check they fit all the criteria. Many people will apply on the chance that you don't really want them to work on Wednesdays and you'll swap it to Thursday to suit them. Make a shortlist of the most suitable and invite them to meet you. You may not like the idea of doing this at home, so see Chapter 4 for alternative venues.

☐ Don't be too disappointed if some don't turn up – if they can't make it to the interview, the chances of them doing a good job were pretty remote. Start the interview by repeating what the vacancy is for, the hours and so on, to flush out any misunderstandings. Listen and observe carefully throughout the conversation so you don't overlook any clues about their suitability or desire to do the job. Don't be won over by offers to leave their present job without working the full notice period – if they are willing to do that to their present employer, they'll do it to you too.

☐ Having seen all the candidates, decide which one seems to be the best option from the perspective of experience, personality, desire to do the job, willingness to learn and any other factors that are important to you. It's hard, if not impossible, to make the 'right' choice; just try for the best choice given what you know and have intuited.

☐ Offer the job to your best choice and arrange when they should start. You may want to wait until they have started before you tell the other candidates they were unsuccessful. If that is impractical, you might want to say that this particular vacancy has been filled, but you will be in touch when another one becomes available.

☐ Get two references, preferably from present and previous employers, or at least from someone you can reasonably rely on to give an honest opinion. If the candidate is unable to provide two referees, I wouldn't take the risk of employing them.

☐ Provide clear and straightforward training on the first and subsequent days, until you are happy that they understand their duties. Training should include directions on how you expect them to behave towards customers, the required standard of appearance and language, standard of driving and vehicles and so on.

☐ From there on, I wish you luck. Management of people is a difficult job. I would like to say that the better you treat your staff, the better they will treat you and the job, but I know that isn't necessarily so. Nor is it an excuse to treat them badly. Everyone has to find their own style and that only comes with experience.

HOW SUPPLIERS AFFECT YOUR PROFESSIONAL IMAGE

It's important for all businesses to get the best possible price for the goods and services they buy, but price is not the only consideration if you want to establish and maintain a good professional reputation. The local business community invariably gets to know who is dealing with whom and it will reflect badly on you if the company you keep is of dubious integrity. Bear these points in mind when choosing and doing business with suppliers.

☐ Take into account factors other than the lowest price. Is the business well established and well thought of? That could be far more valuable to you in the long run.

☐ Pay them on time, and before the due date if your cashflow allows. Prompt payment is always noted and appreciated.

☐ Say thank you for a good service and let them know about problems, not just to gripe, but so they have a chance to put things right.

☐ If you're happy, recommend them to other people. A word-of-mouth referral is the best (and cheapest) way of getting new business and it will be appreciated.

☐ They may in turn recommend you, and if they do, make sure you say thank you.

HOW CLIENTS AFFECT YOUR PROFESSIONAL IMAGE

All self-employed people and small businesses need clients and particularly when you start out, it can be tempting to grab at whatever comes up. My own experience and that of other homeworkers I have spoken to tells me that more is not always better. As well as steering clear of dodgy characters as discussed in the section above on suppliers, working for yourself seems to go better if you follow your gut feelings and only work with people you feel comfortable with.

Sacking the Client

❝ I remember a couple of occasions when I gave notice to a client because I no longer wanted to work with them. The first was in the early days and was a decision made in great trepidation, but the person concerned seemed to be intent on catching out our cleaner by leaving little 'traps' for them, to test their thoroughness and honesty.

113

Evidently the cleaner passed the tests because the client then offered them a job, which would have cost considerably less than employing us.

The other occasion was when the business was better established, but it was an equally nerve-racking decision. One of my largest clients was taken over, and the new owners brought in their own manager to deal with the cleaning. A meeting was arranged for us to discuss the situation, but the manager turned up late without apology or explanation and informed me they wanted a 'cheap job'. I didn't want to lose such a large contract, particularly when previously there had been a good relationship over many years, but it was clear I could not do business on those terms. Lo and behold, a few weeks later I picked up another contract of equal size.

Resources

- ☐ www.chathamhouse.org.uk/about/chathamhouserule
  More information about the origins and use of the Chatham House Rule.

- ☐ www.ico.gov.uk
  The website of the Information Commissioner's Office where you can find more information about handling personal information and if necessary, register as a data controller.

- ☐ *The Pursuit of Wow!: Every Person's Guide to Topsy-turvy Times* by Tom Peters. Random House, 1994.
  This book by one of the most famous of management gurus is now only available secondhand. As Peters is American, so are his case studies and many will be unknown to British readers, but that doesn't matter. It is an accessible read and contains many ideas that small businesses could easily implement to improve their service.

- ☐ www.houseofcolour.co.uk
  Find out what kind of clothes suit your colouring, body shape and personality.

Part 3
Secrets of Success

7
WON'T I FEEL ISOLATED?

In the UK we work the longest hours in Europe, according to the TUC General Secretary Brendan Barber in 2007, so it's not surprising that the people we meet at work are important as colleagues and as friends and prospective partners. If you have always worked with other people, you will naturally wonder about how you will cope when working alone at home.

This chapter covers:

1. How the isolation of working alone, and the way you deal with it, lies at the crux of whether you will enjoy working from home.

2. Passing acquaintances, friends and colleagues can all help to keep you connected, by phone and email as well as meeting face to face. Pets are good company too.

3. Networking gets you out of the house and is a source of help and potential new business. Choose a group carefully and remember everyone was nervous when they first started networking.

4. Online networking can broaden your circle of contacts to cover the globe and offer the possibility of meeting in person too.

Coping with isolation

How you deal with isolation is the key to whether you can happily work from home or not, and all of the homeworkers I spoke to mentioned it as one of the crucial challenges of working from home. There is no-one else around to chat to, discuss the news with, or give you some help when you're feeling stuck.

A Clinical Psychologist's Story

Susan worked in the NHS before starting her own practice: 'I thought I understood about working from home because I'd been a mature student, so I was used to spending hours at my desk at home. But I didn't realise how different it would be to being employed. I hadn't anticipated how much I would miss the interaction with other people. I miss celebrating the little triumphs and having someone to commiserate with me when I'm having a bad day.'

As we found in Chapter 2, how happy you feel working alone will depend on your personality, and largely on whether you are an introvert or extrovert. (If you have not already done so, you might like to complete the questions in Chapter 2 before reading any further.) But no matter how much you enjoy your own company, there will inevitably be times when you want to interact with others. The desire to feel connected with other people is a basic human need.

American psychologist Abraham Maslow published his famous Hierarchy of Needs in the 1950s and it has since become one of the fundamental building blocks of personal development and training. Maslow puts what he calls 'belongingness and love needs' – which include work group, as well as family and other relationships – as the next most important to fulfil after the physical need for air, food, water and shelter, and the 'safety' need for security and stability. In other words, once you are warm, fed and watered, and reasonably sure there aren't any nasty surprises threatening your survival, your most pressing requirement is that of companionship.

The good news is that when you work from home, you don't actually have to work *at* home and you have the freedom to get out and about at any time of day, by planning your work accordingly.

A Trainer's Story

Barry used to be a trainer for a multinational company, based at home on the days he wasn't delivering courses at the corporate training centre. With an outgoing personality, he found himself unable to work at home – there wasn't enough 'buzz'. So he'd take his laptop to local cafes and hotel lobbies with a wireless connection and work there, soaking up the energy of the people around him.

As a homeworker, it is entirely your responsibility to organise regular contact with people who can provide you with the energy and encouragement to keep motivated. I regard this as a top priority, the next most important thing to getting your work done. If you are happy with your own company, it can be tempting to put off meeting other people when you are under pressure, but without some external input, you can quickly lose your momentum.

Just a thought:

The time you think you can't possibly go out is precisely the time you *need* to go out. You will come back feeling much clearer and more enthusiastic about what you need to do. If you stay at your desk you will only fritter away time worrying about how much you have to do and not getting on with it.

An Illustrator's Story

Margaret has worked from home for many years. She writes and illustrates children's books in a studio in her garden in a small seaside town. She appreciates the fact that her job enables her to work from home and to live by the sea: 'Other people probably think I'm so lucky and actually, this must be the best job in the world.'

But for Margaret, the isolation is the hardest thing to deal with. She finds that, with no pressing reason to leave her home and studio: 'It's easy not to make an effort, and then, when I do need to go out, I find I don't want to. When I lived in a small flat in London and worked from home, I almost got agoraphobic. Living in a small town like this can actually be a disadvantage. Because I'm afraid of bumping into people I know when I go out, and ending up wasting time chatting, I don't go. Being on my own so much even affects me when I do go out – as there is normally nobody to talk to, when I do meet people, I tend to rabbit on! Homeworking would never work for someone who can't bear to be alone.'

Staying connected

'Keep in touch!' How often do we say this? And how often do we then neglect to follow it through? Regularly keeping in touch with a group of useful contacts will help you to be successful when you are working from home – some may be able to connect you with other people, some may provide complementary skills to your own, some may come up with good ideas, others may be objective when you can't see the wood for the trees and help you to make a decision. People like this can provide you with a strong and diverse network, so there are huge benefits in keeping up the contact. Building and maintaining a strong network will help you to retain your sanity and perspective when working alone, by providing practical, emotional and intellectual support.

What's a Network?

When I was running my cleaning business, I built up a varied network of people, although I would never have thought about them in those terms. To me they were just nice people I came across in the course of my work, and possibly my social life too, who were able to help me in all kinds of ways, and whom I was also happy to help when I could.

Amongst them I would count people I paid (like my accountant who was always ready to answer annoying questions about the niceties of VAT and tax) or had paid in the past, like a business adviser I worked with for several months. When our contract came to an end, he said I was still welcome to call him if I had any problems I'd like to discuss. He knew by then that I was unlikely to bother him unless I had a serious concern, and no doubt he wanted to keep in touch so he had a good cleaning company to recommend.

Wheels within Wheels

The great thing about networks is that once you've created them, you can tap into your contacts' networks too. The business adviser put me in touch with a friendly solicitor who ended up giving me free advice on employment law on several occasions when staff were misbehaving. The solicitor knew I would mention him to anyone needing legal help, and take my own business to him in future.

Clients and employees were also vital members of my network. Current cleaners who would do some extra hours, plus ex-employees who would occasionally fill in, were invaluable in times of staff shortage. As for clients, I got my second-biggest office cleaning contract by simply mentioning to a client that I was able to take on more work. He mentioned it to a contact who worked in the largest solicitors' practice in Bath, and in due course the business was mine.

And then there were the self-employed friends who would listen to my tales of woe, and give me tea and much-needed commiseration. Just having a good old grumble is sometimes all you need to feel much better!

Make sure you don't just call people when you want something from them (see Chapter 2, Thinking and Feeling), ring just to say hello and ask how things are. Don't wait until there's a crisis, it's too late by then and your network will shrivel pretty quickly if you only ever get in touch to ask favours. Instead make a diary note if time tends to fly by and you forget to do it.

Remember Chapter 2 and think about how your various contacts would like to stay in touch. Would they prefer to have a chat on the phone, meet up for a casual coffee or arrange a more formal meeting to discuss an aspect of work you have in common? Varying the means of communication keeps life interesting for you as well as getting the best from them. The rest of this chapter looks at various ways you can meet people you might want to include in your network. No doubt you will come across many other ways, depending on your profession and personality.

Just a thought:
It's amazing how ideas, which obstinately refused to appear while you were at your desk, will magically appear from nowhere once you start to talk to other people. So many times I've been complaining about a problem I couldn't solve, only to have a solution occur to me before I'd even finished the sentence!

Getting out more

Working in an office, you may have longed to get away from the people crowded into the train, pushing against you in the street or interrupting you at your desk. Working in peace and quiet at home may have seemed the perfect solution. As we've seen in Chapter 5, it can indeed help you be more productive, but when you work at home you will start to appreciate human contact in a way you never did when you were commuting every day. A friend of mine says she knows she's been working alone too long when an interruption like a delivery comes as a welcome break and she starts to make such enthusiastic conversation that the driver edges nervously towards the gate!

A Marketing Manager's Story

Rachel is a self-confessed introvert who loves living in an isolated rural area, so isolated that there are no other houses visible from her windows. But sometimes she only sees her husband and three-year-old from one week to the next and even though she doesn't regard herself as very sociable, at these times she gets desperate for some other company. Fortunately she is on good terms with her neighbours, who welcome her occasional visits.

Having good neighbours to pass the time of day with is a great help when you're working from home, and there are many other ways to brighten up your day with a little light relief. Here are some more suggestions which have worked for me.

LOCAL FACES

Working in an office, you see familiar faces every day – the receptionist, the cleaner, the security guard, the woman who comes in to water the plants. They are probably just the background to other activities. When you work from home, you will have a different set of familiar faces you may well come to value for the diversion they provide. You don't have to go to meetings and events to get your energy renewed and your motivation refuelled. It can happen just by talking to the people you come across in the course of your day. It could be the other parents at the school gates, the man in the newsagents, your hairdresser or the postman.

> **Just a thought:**
> You can get inspiration by talking to people in very different jobs, as they have a totally fresh approach and are unaware of traditional ways of doing things. Even exchanging personal gossip can give you an idea.

FRIENDS AND FAMILY

At the office, the only reminders of family and friends may have been photos on your desk, unless you were able to make personal calls during work time. Of course the people who know you best can provide support and sympathy when you are working from home, and may be crucial in the first few months, but you may have to be disciplined and only contact them outside normal working hours, or you could find that you are inadvertently giving the signal that you are available at any time. In Chapter 8 we look at how to establish boundaries between work time and family time, and how to manage working alongside other family members.

You Need to Get Out More

I've never been a devotee of home improvements, gardening, and so on, and my excuse has always been that my priority on light summer evenings and at weekends is to get out of the house and enjoy a different environment. I meet up with a home-based friend about once a week for coffee. We always go to a café, never each other's houses, so that we can both escape from the familiar four walls. We quickly discovered the places where we can sit for an hour or even two, without being moved on or pressurised into ordering more. Summer is the best time of year— you can sit outside away from the eyes of proprietors intent on turning the tables frequently.

PETS

Being at home all day, you are in the ideal position to keep a pet. Cats and dogs will love you being around more and they are great (and uncritical) companions. In a survey of pet owners carried out in 1999, The Blue Cross animal welfare charity found that 89% of owners believed their pets helped them to relax, 96% thought they combated loneliness and 96% that they provided companionship. They can also help you to establish and keep to a productive work routine (see Chapter 5) and get out of the house regularly. However, it's not a good idea to get a new pet at the same time as beginning to work from home. They are both major changes needing a lot of commitment.

IF YOU ARE EMPLOYED

Think about the people you used to run into in the course of a day in the office, and make the effort to keep as visible as possible. You already have a ready-made network to tap into, made up of colleagues, bosses and team members, so go along to all the normal work events, the Christmas parties, leaving dos, training sessions and meetings. As well as boosting your own morale, it keeps you in the forefront of everyone's mind when you are not physically present in the office every day, a subject covered in Chapter 6. Keeping in touch with former colleagues and bosses when they move to other jobs will expand your circle even further.

A Sales Executive's Story

Sarah sells advertising space in a travel magazine from her home office in the country. Her company's head office, and the rest of her team, is hundreds of miles away, but she is in touch so often by phone and email that they tell her 'they feel like I am on the top floor'. She gets to meet colleagues face to face four or five times a year at trade shows and the industry awards ceremony.

IF YOU ARE SELF-EMPLOYED

You might have to work a little harder at building your network than someone who is employed, so think about all the people you deal with in the course of your work. The list will include your clients, suppliers, employees, people who offer a similar service, and so on. You probably know a number of self-employed people who also work from home. Why not set up a club which meets regularly for lunch or coffee to share news and problems? You can either meet in each others' houses or go to a convenient café.

A Writer's Story

Susy is a writer and editor who belonged to an informal networking group with other freelance mums who lived on the same group of city streets and whose children attended the same school. 'Although we were all doing different jobs, they were all arts based and sometimes introductions within the group led to offers of work. The group provided vital mental and emotional support for the rigours of freelance life and the highlight of our year was the Christmas lunch, which we dressed up for and was so good even PAYE people tried to crash it!'

WORK SUPPORT

In an office environment you are provided with support of all kinds which you never even think about – as well as the social interaction of colleagues at break-times and after-work activities, there is an endless supply of stationery, raw materials and IT support. At home you may have to organise all this for yourself and you might find it becoming more important to actually like the guy who turns up when your computer goes down. Part of the pleasure of the autonomy of working from home is being able to give regular business to those in the same boat.

PHONE AND INTERNET

Although I'd strongly recommend you make a point of arranging regular get-togethers out of the house, of course you don't have to physically meet people to build a supportive network – you can stay at home and use your phone, email and internet forums.

A Web Designer's Story

Alex is a website designer who works from a studio at home and finds that his job can be lonely at times. 'I work better on my own in peace and quiet,' he says, 'but I find I also need other people to bounce ideas off.'

He has used his IT knowledge to establish a virtual office which provides mutual back-up. Using the internet he is in regular contact with a former colleague from the days he worked for someone else, an old school friend from the opposite side of the country, and a lecturer at Porto University in Portugal. These contacts can provide the specialist knowledge he needs and which otherwise would only be available a long journey away.

Once you have been working at home for a while and have established a pattern of phone use, check to make sure you are on the best and cheapest tariff, depending on whether you make a lot of short calls, ring people abroad or are on the phone for periods of an hour or more. You will probably be able to cut back your use of a mobile to the times you have to pop out while expecting a call.

Free online address books and calendars like Plaxo give warning of upcoming birthdays, notify changes in contact details to fellow members and allow you to send ecards. We look at online networking in more detail later in this chapter.

Why is everyone networking?

One way of getting out of the house on a regular basis, and possibly also of generating more business, is to join a networking group. I have noticed that very few people will admit to liking networking – the usual response is a pulled face and a remark like 'Yuck, networking, I hate it, but I suppose you have to do it.'

Maybe this is because so many people associate it with selling and nothing else. They go off to a few organised networking events and are disappointed when they yield no new sales. They then give up and will tell you that 'networking doesn't work'. I suggest that you regard networking purely as a pleasant way of taking a break from work and meeting some new people.

I don't believe networking is about selling, and you will get the best results if you have no expectations in that direction. Many times at networking events I have been enthusiastically hailed by a recent business acquaintance apparently pleased to see me, who then subjects me to a sales pitch. This feels horrible and completely puts me off the individual and their business.

Try to think about networking as all about getting yourself known and liked. This takes time and perseverance, but produces amazing results. You may think you are just not the right kind of person to network. That's what I thought.

I Don't Do Networking

I was lucky in that my cleaning business grew on its own through word of mouth and I never needed to network to get more business. I was always busy working when the events were taking place, and in fact I was often responsible for getting a venue cleaned beforehand and clearing up afterwards, so I got used to being out of sight. When I sold the cleaning company and started out as a business adviser to small businesses, the realisation that my new venture required me to be out 'on show' was a scary one.

With great trepidation I joined the local Chamber of Commerce. Initially I went along with an existing member, the owner of the gym I belonged to, but gradually became confident enough to go alone. Within a few months I had been asked to join the social committee of the Chamber and to do some work for one of the businesses I had come across. Not a bad result for a few evenings spent chatting to new people with a glass of wine in hand.

It was a real revelation to me to find that not only could I do this, but that it could also be enjoyable. It took a while to feel comfortable, but isn't that true of any new activity? The only way it becomes familiar is by getting out there and doing it.

CHOOSING YOUR NETWORKING GROUP

In the last few years there has been a proliferation of networking groups all over the country, and there are now groups for all professions and industries, for women, young businesspeople, the self-employed and those in rural areas, to name just a few.

You can join as a self-employed person or as an employee representing your company. To find out about groups in your area, contact your industry association, the local Chamber of Commerce, your nearest Business Link office, or speak to your business bank manager. There is more information provided in the Resources section at the end of the chapter.

You can network at breakfast, at lunchtime and after work. Some groups simply charge a small fee to cover the cost of room hire and refreshments; others demand a yearly subscription of hundreds of pounds. The latter tend to be more focused on generating business and will offer a limited period where you can try before you buy, so take full advantage and ask some direct questions of a variety of members before you commit.

BNI (Business Networking International), for example, expects members to bring business referrals to each meeting. If you are a one-man band such as a business consultant with a limited amount of specialist clients, you may not have the breadth of contacts to do this. Some networks have very strict rules about attendance and absent members have to find someone else to attend in their place. Standing in for an absent member is an ideal opportunity to try the group out.

Above all, don't be too influenced by promotional material that makes extravagant claims for the amount of extra business the network will generate. Remember the figures quoted may be accurate but they are averages and in my experience some businesses do very well, sometimes to the point of being forced to leave the network because they are swamped by work, whereas others do very poorly and see little or no return on their investment. It can be useful to ask yourself and network members a number of key questions after attending your first event, and certainly before committing yourself.

Questions to ask the network members

☐ How much business have you got by being a member of this network?

☐ What are the features of the group you like and dislike?

☐ What kind of businesses benefit most from this network?

☐ Are there any charges in addition to the subscription?

☐ What happens if I have a grievance or a complaint about another member?

☐ What are the rules on attendance?

☐ What exactly are my obligations if I join this group?

Just a thought:
If you are in any doubt, you might want to contact a recently resigned member to hear their point of view.

Questions to ask yourself before joining a networking group

☐ Was I made to feel welcome by the existing members?

☐ How do I feel about the professionalism of the members? Would I be happy to recommend them to my family and friends or do they only seem interested in making a quick buck? Are these people I would be happy to be associated with?

☐ Was the meeting conducted effectively or was some of the time wasted?

☐ Do the referrals brought by members seem genuine or are they scrabbling to make up the numbers?

☐ Is there anyone belonging to the group who has a natural business synergy with me? Examples of a good business fit that will be able to pass business to each other include web designer and computer hardware consultant, mortgage adviser and will-planning service, graphic designer and printer. If you are a 'one-off' in the group, you may not get many referrals.

STARTING TO NETWORK

Attending your first few networking events can be nerve-racking, and even when you've got some under your belt, you might still find yourself getting a bit nervous. I find that in a fit of enthusiasm I tend to agree to attend an event, and then go off the idea as the day approaches and cast around for reasons why I can't go. I've found that the best thing is to resolutely ignore those doubts, try not to think about it, and just turn up as arranged. I have never once regretted the decision, even when I was worried about sparing the time. These are my tried and tested tips for quickly feeling at ease.

☐ Until you get used to networking, go with someone you know, preferably someone experienced at networking who will introduce you to other people. Or arrange to meet an associate there, so that you will know at least one person.

☐ If you do know people at the event, be very disciplined and try not to succumb to the temptation to talk to them all the time – after all, you are there to meet new contacts.

☐ If you are arriving alone, as you enter, ask the person greeting arrivals to introduce you to someone you specifically want to meet or someone from a particular industry you would like to make contact with.

☐ Remember that the other people at the event are likely to be as nervous as you, or will remember that they used to feel nervous. They are as keen to find someone to talk to as you are.

☐ Never feel you can't approach someone, no matter how influential they may be – they are there to meet people too and you may be just the person they are looking for.

☐ It can be difficult to focus your attention on your current companion when so much is going on around you, especially when you know you must move on soon. So try not to be a 'meerkat' – don't gaze over their shoulder around the room and make your companion feel belittled.

☐ The most difficult thing at a network event is being left alone when everyone else is chatting away in groups of two or three. Don't hesitate, join a group straightaway. A threesome is better, as one of them is probably feeling less involved than the others and will welcome your arrival.

☐ Sometimes your conversation will reach a natural end but you can't think of a polite way to move on. Don't be stranded with the same person for the whole event – say something like 'It's been great to meet you and I hope we'll bump into each other again, but I mustn't monopolise you.' Ask them if they can introduce you to someone else.

Just a thought:

Are you worried about being left alone at a networking event? Try picking up a plate of snacks from the buffet table and offering them to people who look interesting. If you strike up a conversation, you can put the plate down or share it with your new friend.

FOLLOWING UP AFTER NETWORKING

With any luck you will have enjoyed your time at the group, but don't just forget about it once you get home, particularly if during the course of a conversation you promised to send someone some information. A little time spent following up can produce great results:

☐ The day after the event, send an email to each person you met, saying how good it was to meet them. Sometimes people attach information about their business to this email, but as I don't believe networking is about selling, I find this irritating. Use your judgement as to whether this is appropriate.

☐ Scribble some notes on the back of each card you collected to remind you what you talked about, and file the cards, noting the date and occasion. You can have a quick look at them before the next event. People are always pleased to be remembered.

☐ If you think of any information, like a website or an article, which might be useful to someone you met, send it on to them. If you are willing to help others without expecting anything in return, you will build a strong network.

☐ Diary further contact according to the situation and the personality of your contact. Have a look at Chapter 2, page 28 if you are wondering whether a card, phone call or meeting would be most suitable.

Online networking

Joining a local networking group means you make new contacts in your local area. Join an online network and you will be in touch with people from all over the world, people you would otherwise never have the chance to meet. Business networks you might like to check out include LinkedIn, Xing, Ecademy and Ryze. Facebook and MySpace, well known for social networking, are now also being used by businesspeople. I have come across both devotees of online networking and those who don't quite get the point. Your own reaction may depend on how much you enjoy online activity. If you're the kind of person who can't wait to get away from the computer when you've finished work, online networking probably isn't for you, although many online groups offer face-to-face events as well. Here are a few points to bear in mind before committing yourself.

☐ Start with large, well established groups like Ecademy and LinkedIn and check them out as a guest. Large networks have special interest clubs you can join, or you could look for a specialist network related to your industry or interests.

☐ The same principle applies to online networking as to anything in life – the more you put in, the more you are likely to get out. It's therefore likely to be time consuming, at least in the beginning. You will be required to provide your personal details and a profile about your life and career.

☐ Tempting as it is to slap something up and get on with networking straightaway, take care in writing your profile to be concise and interesting, and then check it for spelling and grammar mistakes. This is your introduction to the world of networkers and they will make judgements about you accordingly. As time goes on and your work develops, remember to keep updating your profile.

☐ Be prepared for a flood of welcome emails from keen networkers who contact each new member in order to expand their own network. A standard email will save you time when replying unless an individual is of particular interest to you and warrants a tailored response.

☐ Online networks operate on the principle that the more contacts you have the better. Thomas Power, the founder and Chairman of Ecademy, claims that if you have 1000 people in your network, you'll earn £100,000 a year. However attractive a proposition that is, be careful to balance time building your network with time spent getting your work done and with maintaining your local network.

☐ It's easier to be harsh or critical online than face to face, and often hard to judge the intended tone of an email you receive, so don't send impulsive emails. Better to leave some time and re-read your draft before sending. Also remember that any online communication may be read by many others, not just the original intended recipients. That may include your clients, bosses and people of influence in your industry.

☐ Some smaller networks exist purely to help out members through the exchange of information. When Clare relocated her business from the city to the country (see Chapter 1) she was able to recruit three well qualified employees simply by posting an email on her local network for women in business, making a significant saving in advertising costs.

The Stories of Two Trainers

John is a trainer and coach based just outside London who has been a member of Ecademy for several years. He uses activity on the Ecademy website as a way to ease into work (see Chapter 5) and belongs to some of the Ecademy special interest clubs. Although no work has yet come his way as a result of his membership, he sees it as a way of getting to know some interesting, like-minded people who might generate opportunities for him in the future. Through Ecademy he has connected with professionals in his field who work abroad and who will be handy contacts if he is ever visiting their area.

Martin, on the other hand, a trainer and writer, has been offered a book contract by a fellow member of Ecademy who spotted that Martin's experience fitted his requirements and got in touch. Both online and face-to-face networking can pay unexpected dividends at any time!

Resources

☐ Your local café – preferably with good coffee, homemade cakes and a free wireless connection, so you can work there when you're fed up at home, and have somewhere to meet friends and business associates.

☐ *Feel the Fear and Do It Anyway*, by Susan Jeffers, Vermilion, 2007.
This is the twentieth anniversary edition of the classic self-help book which explodes the myth that successful people are fearless – they're not, they just get on and do it anyway, and so can you.

☐ www.brnet.co.uk
Business Referral Exchange, a national organisation which hosts weekly local meetings.

☐ www.bni-europe.com/uk
Business Network International, run though local weekly 'chapters'.

☐ www.theathenanetwork.com
A women's business network that holds meetings at lunchtime, so ideal if you can't commit to regular breakfast meetings. Find your nearest group on the website. The network is run on a franchise basis, so may also be a business opportunity.

☐ www.wireuk.org
Women in Rural Enterprise – a networking specifically for self-employed women in the country.

☐ www.enterprisenation.com
Register on this site to receive e-news and podcasts about working from home and to make posts on the forums.

☐ www.fsb.org.uk
The Federation of Small Businesses represents over 200,000 businesses across the UK and lobbies government on their behalf. As a member you have access to a 24-hour legal helpline and local meetings.

☐ www.chamberonline.co.uk
Find your local Chamber of Commerce.

☐ www.plaxo.com
An online address book service. When you update your contact details, all those connected to you are automatically informed.

ONLINE NETWORKING SITES

☐ www.ecademy.com
Based in the UK, Ecademy describes itself as a 'social network' for businesspeople with over 150,000 members worldwide. It offers several grades of membership, at corresponding cost, and organises talks and events for members.

☐ www.facebook.com
Previously known as a social network, Facebook is now being used by businesspeople too.

☐ www.linkedin.com
You can join LinkedIn for free and invite people you know to 'connect' with you. There are 12 million members worldwide, representing 150 industries.

☐ www.ryze.com

☐ www.xing.com

8

HOW DO I SEPARATE WORK AND HOME?

People often choose to work from home for a better work/life balance, but when work and family life happen in the same place, it can be hard to establish boundaries for each. You will find when your work is based at home that your concept of 'home' changes. No longer is it a place of refuge from the madness of life, a place where you can close the door, relax and be yourself, but the place where you also have to deal with all aspects of work, including the mundane and exasperating.

This chapter covers:

1. How to look after your own emotional, mental and physical health.

2. How to nurture your relationships with family and friends.
   (These sections complement Chapter 5, which is about creating a structure for your day and working effectively from home, so are best read in conjunction with it.)

3. Adapting your relationship with your partner, whether they go out to work or also work from home.

4. Ways of creating and keeping boundaries for children and teenagers.

5. How to cope when coming into your home is the experience your customers are paying for.

Taking care of yourself while working from home

LOOKING AFTER YOURSELF EMOTIONALLY AND MENTALLY

When you go out to work, not only do you put a physical distance between your home and the office, but you also set up a useful emotional and mental distance by putting on your work persona along with your work clothes and spending the day 'in character', whether you are a secretary, designer or builder. Your work persona gives you an element of emotional protection and enables you to shrug off some of the petty or disturbing things that happen to you at work. When you get home, you shed the work persona and the protective shell along with your clothes, take down the guard and get back to being the 'real' you relating to family and friends.

You are more vulnerable when you work at home, because you lack that protective shell; you could have been putting the washing out just moments before that difficult client called to berate you. Problems you might have dismissed easily in the office can get under your skin and upset you, and you can start to feel that you and your home are being infected by the moods and problems of your associates.

Conversely going out to work can be a relief if there are problems at home. Getting away for the day can help to take your mind off your troubles and put things in perspective. Staying put, on the other hand, constantly reminds you of what's going wrong and might also put you in constant contact with the person(s) you would like to see less of. Added to which you are working in a familiar environment where many things could trigger a dip in mood – realising nobody has cleared up their breakfast things or getting a call from your mother at the wrong time can put you in a negative frame of mind just when you need to be upbeat.

CHANGING YOUR MOOD

To get the best work results you need to be as positive and confident as possible, so it's vitally important that you are aware of your emotional and mental states and able to exert some control over them. The key is to become aware of your mood and understand that you can move on from blaming other people for upsetting you and change your state of mind into one that is more useful, whether you need to make a phone call or write a report. We're not taught to do this as children and so at first it can seem too difficult to overcome all those years of habitual behaviour, but it's only a question of practice.

You might realise that you need to shift from feeling upset and down to positive and self-assured. Think about the last time you felt really confident and remember in detail exactly what that felt like. Make the experience as real as possible – remember what you were wearing, where you were, who was there, what you and they were saying, and what you were saying to yourself. Use all your senses – how the food tasted if you were eating, whether you could smell someone's perfume, the texture of the chair you were sitting in.

The mind can't tell the difference between reality and imagination so just thinking about it will bring about the same feelings of confidence. As you imagine the scene, don't picture yourself in it but see it through your own eyes, as if you are really there now and observing everything exactly as it was. As you practise this you will start to get those confident feelings again and in time you will only have to think about that event to restore your confidence.

If you're really feeling down in the dumps you might not be able to remember a time when you felt like that, so instead *imagine* how it must feel. Otherwise you could think about someone who personifies confidence and imagine what they do and feel to be that way.

KNOWING HOW TO REACT WHEN SOMEONE UPSETS YOU

It's natural to make assumptions about people on the basis of the way they behave. Maybe you feel that someone just spoke to you very brusquely on the phone. Your reaction will probably be to think that either they are very rude, in which case you don't like them much, or to assume that for some reason *they* don't like *you*. Either way, the encounter might put you in a negative mood but both may be completely wide of the mark.

Stephen Covey tells a story about this in his bestselling book *The Seven Habits of Highly Effective People*. He was on the subway in New York when a man got on with his two children. The man sat down next to him and closed his eyes, while his children ran riot around the carriage. Finally Covey could bear it no more and asked the man to control them. The man opened his eyes and replied that he knew he should do something, but they had come directly from the hospital where his wife had just died, and he was at a loss to know what to do. As you can imagine, Covey's irritation vanished in a second.

So why not assume the best about people if they don't deal with you as you'd like? Give them the benefit of the doubt and assume they've just had some bad news or they are having an awful day.

FEELING GUILTY

Susy relocated from central London to a country cottage, where her office is next to the conservatory. Sounds wonderful, but in fact she says that whenever she is working, she is reminded that the garden needs sorting out, and vice versa.

One of the worst aspects of working from home is that having achieved something at work, you step out of your workspace and are reminded that the washing up needs doing, the grass is too long or the food cupboard is empty. But if you spend too long sorting that out, you start thinking of the work you're neglecting in your office.

Although I say it with trepidation, and I don't want to get into the old multi-tasking argument, women do seem to suffer from this ever-present guilt more acutely than men, especially when children are thrown into the mix. Men seem to be able to concentrate exclusively on one thing at a time, whereas women juggle lots, if only in their heads.

Another odd kind of guilt that afflicts homeworkers who used to go out to work is the feeling that being able to work at home is such a privilege that they have to pay for it in some way, to justify its benefits, although they're not sure to whom: themselves, their partners or their bosses. They suddenly have all the time that used to be spent travelling and feel it must be used properly. I think this is one of the reasons homeworkers are so much more productive.

It seems that feeling guilty is just one of the side effects of working from home that you have to get used to, and it does lessen with practice.

GETTING SUPPORT

No matter how contented you are with your own company, from time to time you will need the company and stimulation of being around other people. If you haven't already done so, have a look at Chapter 7 for ideas on getting out and meeting people.

KNOWING WHEN AND HOW TO SWITCH OFF

Having your work easily accessible to you at home can make it hard to stop when you should, and to switch off thoughts of work during downtime. It's easier if you plan in advance the time you intend to stop working and then keep to it, even if you're tempted to plough on. This is a knack homeworkers tend to learn by experience, usually by overdoing things and then realising it's doing them no good. It helps to make a point of switching off the computer and turning down the volume of the answer phone if you can, so that your relaxation isn't disturbed by incoming calls. However, with all the technology at our disposal – mobile, BlackBerry, wireless networks – you can be almost anywhere and still have a call or email come in. Switching off completely may be very hard if you're in a business where customers might ring up at any time to ask for your help with an emergency.

> **Just a thought:**
> 'When you work from home, you're never not at work.'
> Claire, who does the admin for her husband's roofing business

Sometimes switching off is not an option because work and life are inextricably intertwined.

A Farmer's Story

John grew up on the family farm and has never had another job. For him, his work is about maintaining an asset to pass on to the next generation, and he makes no distinction between work and pleasure: 'I do a lot of hours, but I don't necessarily regard it as work.

My definition of work is whether or not I'd have to pay another person to do a job. If I go off for a shoot, I'm keeping the vermin down, but I don't regard that as work. Cutting cauliflowers in winter, though, that's graft.'

Or you might find that the boundaries between work and relaxation become blurred in a positive way once you start working from home and your attitudes to 'work time' and 'relaxation time' are different. This is how it changed for Susan.

A Pyschologist's Story

'When I worked at the hospital I finished at 5 o'clock and I'd go home and veg out for the evening. If I'd had to take work home, I'd have been very resentful. Now my life is much more balanced and I have more freedom. If I want to meet a friend during the day, I'll do some work in the evening instead. It's a completely different thing and I don't resent working in the evening at all.'

LOOKING AFTER YOURSELF PHYSICALLY

Working from home means you lose the external discipline that makes you get up, dress for work, leave the house on time and eat at fixed break times, so many people fear that staying in the house all day, with constant access to food and drink, will make them overweight and slothful. Making sure you look after your physical health is part of the discipline of working from home, but it doesn't have to be any harder than resisting cakes and crisps in the office.

Diet

Your proximity to the fridge and food cupboard could become a problem. It's all too easy to make snacking and cups of coffee a regular feature of your working day and to resort to them when you run out of inspiration or as a reward for completing a tricky assignment. Here's how to work from home and not put on weight:

☐ It's a well known tip, but it really does help if you avoid food shopping when you're hungry. A rumbling stomach makes your favourite treats and the current BOGOFs hard to resist.

☐ It's much easier to leave all those goodies on the supermarket shelf than it is to resist munching your way through them once you've got them home. You know your weaknesses, so if necessary avoid that part of the shop altogether.

☐ If you're close to succumbing, imagine that as soon as you get to the checkout you're going to bump into the last person you'd want to meet with all those indulgences in your basket. Maybe your slender and immaculate neighbour, your personal trainer or a member of your exercise class.

☐ As always, self-knowledge is key, so notice the times of day you feel most hungry and the times you are most tempted to nibble on fatty or sugary snacks. You can then plan your eating patterns accordingly. You might not want much breakfast but be starving by lunchtime. Having your main meal of the day then, and a light snack later will help to keep weight off.

☐ Don't cut out your favourite fattening foods entirely or the feeling of being denied might lead to a binge. Indulge in a controlled way, such as having a piece of cake when you go out for a coffee rather than buying a whole cake to take home. It's easier to control your intake when you're eating with other people – nobody wants to be seen as greedy.

☐ As a last resort, if you do have tempting foods at home and you don't trust your own willpower, there's no shame in asking your partner to hide and ration them.

Exercise

☐ If your work demands a lot of sitting down, get up and walk around regularly or you can gradually become increasingly hunched which in turn leads to a downturn in spirits. Getting out into the fresh air will give a boost to both body and mind. Sue says she is 'chomping at the bit' to get out of the house at the end of the working day, and she goes to three exercise classes a week: 'I may not speak to anyone while I'm there, but I really look forward to stretching and pushing myself. I'm the fittest I've ever been.'

☐ Building an exercise class or session at the pool or gym into your working routine means you are more likely to keep up regular exercise. Unlike your office-bound colleagues, you can go to sports facilities at quiet times during the day and to all kinds of daytime classes.

☐ You can use exercise as the start of your day and/or to signal the time you are switching off by walking round the block or taking the dog out.

☐ A rebounder (mini trampoline) is a great way of getting exercise without even having to put on your shoes and leave the house, so it's ideal in winter. It's also a quick and effective way to get out of a bad mood – just bounce from irritation into cheerfulness. Playing upbeat music as you bounce keeps the momentum going and quickly lifts your mood.

Re-energisers

Sometimes you just need a quick energy boost to keep you going until you've achieved the deadline or got the letter in the post. You don't have to rely on caffeine or even leave your desk.

☐ Press the middle of your palm with the thumb of your other hand to give yourself a shot of energy when you're drooping. If you're feeling flexible you can do the same thing by pressing below the ball of your foot.

☐ Eyes get tired looking at the computer for long periods so make a habit of blinking regularly and to rest them, look out of the window into the distance and then look at something close up, like your hand.

☐ Breathe! Take three deep breaths, not just into your chest but deep down into your lungs. Or try the cleansing breath used in yoga to get rid of toxins and oxygenate the brain – breathe in for a count of 4, hold the breath for 2, breathe out for 6, hold for 2 and repeat.

☐ Stimulate the acupuncture points on your ears by taking hold of the top of your ears and pulling them up. Work all around the edge until you get down to the lobes. Pull them down sharply and release.

☐ Tension can build up in your jaw, so open your mouth in a wide yawn while saying 'Aaah' and massaging the hinge of your jawbone up near your ears.

Physical therapies

Massage, reflexology, shiatsu and many other therapies are physically and mentally beneficial for homeworkers and are a great way to switch off at the end of the week or reward yourself for finishing a major project.

Therapists often swap sessions between themselves in order to keep developing their skills and may well be open to the idea of swapping their expertise with yours, a massage or series of massages for some book-keeping work, for example.

Illness

If you work away from home and you're feeling a bit off-colour, it's easy to ring in sick. Nobody knows how ill you are and you'll still get paid after all. You might think homeworkers would be even more tempted to stay in bed, but in fact the opposite is true. As mentioned in the section above on feeling guilty, homeworkers seem to feel the privilege of working from home gives them something to prove, and if you're self-employed, you may well not earn anything while off sick, so the incentive to keep working is even stronger.

It's certainly possible to keep working between naps and doses of medication – and I've done just that while suffering from a kidney infection, although now I think I must have been mad – but taking a few days off would allow your mind and body the time to recover more quickly. The best guide is to ask yourself, 'If I were working outside my home and suffering from this illness, would I stay off work?' and act accordingly.

Managing family and friends

Much as you love your family and friends and enjoy their company, you might find you need to put some ground rules in place to make sure they understand you are working even if you happen to be at home. To gently help them get the idea they should not regularly turn up or ring during the working day you might try the following suggestions:

- ☐ If you have separate home and business lines it is probably easier to keep the answer phone on the home line during the day and only return calls after work.

- ☐ If you only have one phone line, always answer it during the day with a formal business greeting. With luck this should immediately indicate to family and friends that you are on duty and not to be disturbed by social matters.

- ☐ If they seem bent on chatting, tell them you have a deadline to meet or are expecting an important call and will call them back after you have finished work for the day.

- ☐ When you need to end a call without delay and without offending, the lines 'I'd better let you go' or 'I mustn't keep you' work well, implying that you are the one who might be a nuisance, not them.

- ☐ If someone turns up unexpectedly at your door, greet them with something along the lines of 'How lovely to see you and such a shame I can't invite you in. I've got a deadline to meet and I'm behind already. Can I call you later to make some proper arrangements?' If you reluctantly let them in and start chatting it's much more difficult to dispatch them gracefully.

- ☐ Some people recommend opening the door with a mobile or cordless phone clamped to your ear, but I only ever do it if I really am on a call, in case someone chooses just that minute to ring me!

- ☐ If you do ever arrange to meet up with a friend or family member in normal working hours, make it clear that this is because you are on holiday or having a day off and tell them the date that the usual arrangements will resume.

(If you haven't yet read Chapter 5 on making a structure for your day and being productive at home, it might help to have a look at it now as much of the material there is complementary to this.)

Looking after your main relationship

Just a thought:
Although I refer to 'your partner' throughout this section, the following points are also relevant if other close family members work from home, especially if you work in a family business.

You know those statistics that claim to calculate the stress levels of life events such as divorce, bereavement and moving house? As far as I know nobody has yet attempted to work out the level of stress incurred by you or your partner starting to work from home, but you should regard it as a major life change and plan accordingly. The change to working from home may alter your respective roles in ways you don't anticipate and it's important to realise that you may not reach equilibrium straightaway.

A Market Researcher's Story

When Sue and her husband both worked away from home they shared household jobs roughly 50/50 and whoever got in first started the dinner. Sue assumed that was the way modern relationships worked. Then she started to work from home and found herself taking a much more traditional wifely role and doing all the housework and cooking, because she was around to do it: 'There were no major rows, but I did go through a period of resentment about it. I felt my working from home was very beneficial for my husband as I was here to do the errands and he didn't have to do any of that anymore.'

Things didn't fall into place immediately but now they have a cleaner and Sue continues to do the washing and cooking as well as her paid work. She finds it strange that they have fallen into what she had always seen as a stereotypical division of the household labour, and that they are both very happy with the situation: 'The thing is that it works, and also I feel like I'm beating the system. I'm doing a well paid job, but I have time to do housewifely things like baking cakes as well and I actually enjoy it.'

Working at home tends to magnify what is going on in your relationship already, so that small irritations become more important and can blow up out of all proportion. Just as communications in the form of computers and phones are vital to the ability to work from home, communication is also key to looking after your personal relationships when you do so. Manage the transition to homeworking as smoothly as possible by following these suggestions.

☐ You may have dreamt of this moment for a long time, but like any other major change, it may take a while to get settled in, so make allowances for everyone in the meantime.

☐ Think in detail about the many changes that working from home will bring to your household and the way you run it. Go through your normal working day and identify who will do what, whether it's getting breakfast, taking the children to school, doing the washing, ironing, meal planning, shopping, cooking, washing up, cleaning and so on.

A Farmer's Story

John and Hayde have been happily married for 12 years and have two children. He says 'There are farmers' wives – and my mother was a farmer's wife – and there are wives of farmers, and Hayde is one of the latter. She isn't interested in farming and never has been, but that doesn't matter because we split responsibilities. I make decisions about the farm and she's in charge of the house and that works well for us.'

☐ Having agreed responsibility for each job, you might need to be flexible in practice, if circumstances and pressure of work demand that responsibilities are changed from time to time.

☐ Try not to 'keep score' – 'I've been doing the cooking all week and you're just sitting there in front of the television.' Dwelling on how much you're doing and how little your partner does makes you bitter and judgemental, and somehow whenever I've succumbed to it, I discover I have overlooked a generous, selfless act and put myself even more into the doghouse. Don't chance it.

☐ Do, however, air resentments as soon as they emerge. Don't wait until you can't hold it in any longer and it explodes in an outburst, even if you feel that saying anything will make you look petty or childish. Try putting it like this – 'I know this isn't logical/rational/grown-up, but I feel resentful/envious/cross about you going on that business trip/leaving early in the morning so I have to get the kids ready/be here all the time on my own.' Just getting these corrosive little thoughts out in the open can make the situation feel much better, while letting them fester creates more poison.

☐ Find out how your partner likes to be asked to do something and what drives them up the wall. Out of a fear of seeming bossy, I have a tendency to ask for something in an oblique way – 'I'm getting hungry now, are you?' which translated means 'Please will you get lunch ready because I'm concentrating on this and I need food very soon or I'll get extremely grumpy.' My partner finds that annoying, and if he's feeling contrary he will just agree that yes, he's getting a bit peckish, and carry on with his work, because I didn't actually ask him to do anything, did I? Clearing up these little points of aggravation will save a lot of time and many lost tempers.

GIVING AND RECEIVING FEEDBACK

Discussing all these matters demands honest communication, and that can be difficult even, and sometimes especially, with those who are closest to us. One way to help establish good communication and keep it flowing is to learn how to give and receive feedback. By feedback I don't just mean criticism of your partner's behaviour or performance, even though from time to time you may want to offer that. I'm talking about exchanging views and feelings about your roles and lives so that life for both of you and the rest of the family is as well organised and as enjoyable as possible. Here are some basic ground rules about feedback that will stop the process becoming a flash point.

- ☐ It's essential you both agree to giving and receiving feedback or it will simply be a cause of conflict. It can be a risky business because often you are pointing out a blind spot – a characteristic your partner is genuinely unaware of – and unwanted observations can be hurtful and destructive.

- ☐ Agree on how to do it and choose the right time and place – going for a walk can be useful as you are side by side, perhaps in step as well, so it's less confrontational. When we lived in Cornwall we often drove to the beach for a meeting and to report back on how we were doing. Being outside can open up your mind and allow in new ideas and possibilities.

- ☐ If you want to give feedback about a specific event, do it as soon as possible afterwards. There is something about the human mind that is willing to accept constructive criticism immediately after an event, but starts to rationalise and justify as time passes.

- ☐ Keep your feedback strictly about the issue and don't mix it up with personal issues e.g. 'I'd like you to do more around the house so I can start work quicker in the mornings' rather than 'I'm sick of you never helping me in the house. It's your mother's fault; she spoilt you rotten' etc.

- ☐ Be aware that listening to understand is so much better for communication than listening for a pause so you can get your point in. You can make your point when you have listened your partner out; in fact, if you listen well, you may not need to make that point because you will have discovered the root of the issue is something else entirely.

☐ Your partner is very aware of your strengths and weaknesses and so is in an ideal position to point them out. They will also know if you are overusing a strength to the point that it becomes a weakness. For example, a wish to maintain harmony between members of a team can be a drawback if it results in reluctance to confront a member about poor performance.

☐ Always challenge the behaviour and not the person. For example 'That wasn't a particularly helpful response to the situation' rather than 'Why are you being so bolshie?'

☐ Concentrate on the effect that behaviour had on you – 'When you said that to the customer it made me feel really small' instead of 'Why are you always running me down in front of customers?'

☐ Once again, remember that this isn't just a process for giving negative feedback. Make a point of mentioning all the things your partner does that are helpful and considerate and your communication will proceed much more smoothly.

WHEN YOUR PARTNER WORKS AT HOME TOO

The old saying that goes 'I married you for life, but not for lunch' was once used primarily by wives whose husbands had retired and were cluttering up the house during the day, but now it could be a piece of advice for couples who both work from home. If you have been used to being apart all day and getting together over dinner to discuss your day, it can be a shock to both be in the house all day. My partner has, at different times, worked in an office, been away for the whole of the working week, and worked full time at home, and these are my suggestions for keeping a relationship in good shape while both working at home.

☐ Have separate offices, preferably out of earshot of each other, so you can work in your own idiosyncratic ways without interrupting each other.

☐ If you share the computer or other equipment, plan in advance who will do what and when, so that you don't waste time hanging around waiting for them to finish.

☐ Respect your partner's way of working, particularly if it is different to your own and particularly if they are involved in creative work. Even sticking your head round the door when they are 'in the flow' and asking 'Fancy a coffee?' might interrupt their train of thought.

☐ Don't try to be 'together' too much – your pace of work might not match theirs so don't feel guilty if you take breaks at different times.

☐ Too much time together can lead to staleness and put a strain on a relationship. Having separate hobbies and friends and making a point of going out separately means you both have interests outside the house and have news to tell each other when you do get together.

WHEN YOUR PARTNER WORKS FROM HOME IN THE SAME BUSINESS

If working from home tends to magnify what is already happening in a relationship, then working together in the same business magnifies it many times over. In the words of Jane, who runs a B&B: 'Working together can be very testing on a marriage but Peter and I work well together. We both tend to be a bit perfectionist and so our standards are similar. We only fall out when we're tired – you can't snap at the guests so we snap at each other, but we can recognise it now.'

When things are going well, running a business together can be rewarding in many respects and bring you and your partner closer together. If things are not going so well, along with the strains on the business and relationship, you may have money worries to cope with, especially if the business is your sole source of income. Money issues are a major cause of tension within relationships and are one of the points you should look at carefully before going into business together.

☐ How are you going to divide up the workload? The best scenario is where you have complementary talents, for example, he is good at going out and getting the job done and she is good at admin. and customer relations. It helps to have a good knowledge of your personalities and natural capabilities, so examine your strengths and decide who will do what. Write down a list of all the tasks required to run the business and allocate them to each person depending on what they are good at. If you're not sure or you want to develop skills not yet utilised, consider getting a personality profile done. People are amazed at their accuracy and they help to identify latent talent.

☐ It's important to understand your attitudes towards risk. It could be a major problem if whenever there is an opportunity to expand or do something different one of you is gung ho and the other is cautious. If your attitudes to risk are very different you will both be happier doing different things.

☐ It's also important to agree on how much money you need to take out of the business for your living expenses and what it's to be spent on. Again, if your priorities are vastly different it will be better for your relationship to earn and spend your incomes separately.

☐ Remember to keep redefining your working relationship. Just because when you started out she did all the networking and you did the technical work doesn't mean it has to be that way forever. Try different things out and see how it works. If nothing else, a change in routine can generate new ideas and get you out of a rut.

☐ Don't talk about business all the time. It's difficult to resist if you suddenly have a brilliant idea in the bath or doing the washing up, but try to save it as you would if you worked away from home – I doubt you'd ring your boss late at night to tell them about your latest brainwave.

☐ Remember that you are in a relationship outside work and take time to nurture that as well as the business by having regular evenings out and weekends away. (You may well get ideas for your business by visiting restaurants, hotels and shops, but put your relationship first while you're away.)

☐ Ideally you will be able to give each other moral support and when one is down the other will provide reassurance.

WHEN YOUR PARTNER DOES NOT WORK

If your partner does not work, it might be a shock for them to have someone at home all day when previously they had the house to themselves, even if you are shut away behind a closed door. A little give and take may be required while adjustments are made to the new arrangements.

Children and homeworking

Many people start to think about working from home when they first have children and want to spend more time with them. In theory it sounds like the ideal way of getting the most from your professional and domestic lives, but in practice it can be a tricky juggling act to perform.

On the positive side, a child growing up with a parent working from home may benefit by absorbing the connection between work and money, and possibly learning to be entrepreneurial themselves.

The Story of a Budding Entrepreneur

Martin's daughters are disappointed when they are at home and he is out working on a plumbing job, but they also understand this means he is earning money for the family. Their seven-year-old daughter recently asked him over dinner whether he 'made up' the prices for his customers. On being told that he did indeed work out the price for each job, she asked why he couldn't simply charge more and make more money! Quite an insight for a seven-year-old.

However, if you are self-employed and building up a successful business is necessarily your first priority, you may feel that family life suffers as a result.

A B&B Owner's Story

Jane's parents divorced and her mother ran a hairdressing business to support them. 'If ever I complained about not having her attention, she made it very clear that her work was our bread and butter. Luckily our children were older when we started our business but I'm sure there are things we haven't done as a family because of not getting regular days off.'

WORKING FROM HOME WITH CHILDREN

Fitting work around childcare is easier when they are still babies as you can work around their naps, although of course this limits the amount of time available to maybe four or five hours a day at most (not taking into account how tired you might be looking after a new baby). Small children may demand your attention at the very time you need to concentrate on work.

A Book-keeper's Story

Annie does her work while her ten-year-old son is at school and the baby is asleep, which generally gives her about four hours work time during the day. She may also work again in the evening after bedtime. In the school holidays she works while her son is playing with friends and again in the evenings.

You will need to find your own ways of getting your work done and devoting time to your children, but other people's experience may help.

☐ You may find that you have conflicting loyalties and decide to accept it is impossible to 'have it all'.

An Event Organiser's Story

'After the birth of my first child, I went back to my full-time job with a racing team and the baby went to nursery all day. When the job came to an end and I was offered a similar role by another employer, I agonised over whether to take it or to do fewer hours. It was an awful decision to make but in the end I had to accept that now I was a mother, I was not the person I was before, and I'll never be the same again, because now I have the

responsibility of children.' Nicki presently works 15 hours a week and plans to increase her workload as her children grow up.

- ☐ Small children don't understand the concept of 'Don't disturb Daddy; he's working'. One homeworker I know put a lock on his workspace door to stop his children interrupting him, but that wouldn't work for all children.

- ☐ Work flexible hours, when the children are at nursery or school, and in the evening after they have gone to bed.

- ☐ Take it in turns with family and friends to provide childcare. Nicki does her best not to pay for childcare as the cost would eat so far into her earnings. Instead she organises what she calls 'favour swaps' with her friends and family. She looks after her cousin's children one day a week and her cousin takes hers for a day, so that they each have a day clear.

- ☐ Depending on your business, it might be much less stressful to be open with your clients.

A Web Designer's Story

'If your work is good and your prices are competitive, the fact that you are working from home and have small children shouldn't be a problem,' says Alex, who is self-employed. 'My clients understand. They are human beings, after all, and some have children too. I take my four-year-old to meetings with my oldest clients and they don't mind at all. I'm lucky in that respect and I realise it might be very different if I had a corporate job.'

(If you are unsure how to juggle children and professional commitments, it might help to read Chapter 4 on deciding whether to hold meetings at home and Chapter 6 on maintaining a professional image.)

- ☐ It might be prudent to keep your computer passwords out of the hands of your children or they could unintentionally get you into a lot of trouble, as Hilary found.

A Development Manager's Story

Hilary used to work in the family living room, where she kept her work computer. One day she was unexpectedly called into the office and asked to bring the computer with her. She was questioned by two strangers who told her that someone had been viewing inappropriate images and sending chain letters on the computer, which was taken away for investigation. Hilary was in shock and the whole family under suspicion, until eventually her young son admitted that he had gone to the sites under peer pressure. Hilary was suspended for a month and feared for her job but was eventually reinstated. She has since heard of people who have been sacked after many years service for letting someone else use their computer or for using their work computer for personal purposes within work hours, often not even realising they shouldn't do it. She hopes others will learn from her own horrible experience and never give away their passwords.

Working from home when you have teenagers

Small children may demand more of your time, but they are more biddable and easier to keep to a regular routine, whereas teenagers can be an unpredictable and somewhat volatile force in the environment where you are trying to be professional.

A Business Writer's Story

Caroline is well acquainted with the difficulties of working with a teenager in the background: 'At that age they become very self-centred, the centre of their own universe. Everything that happens is a crisis they want to involve you in. They will crash in from school, loudly recounting what's happened during the day, and want instant attention. They leap for the phone in case it's a call for them and constantly want to make outgoing calls. I've tried to establish boundaries but they're hopeless at keeping to them, as they either don't, or won't, realise the impact they have on people around them. They're also bad at conforming to adult-imposed routines, which makes working in the school holidays difficult as I never know when I'll get a good stretch of time to myself.'

There are no easy solutions. Your personality, your teenager's personality, your family circumstances, where your office is in the house – all these factors make your situation unique and demand different responses. That said, here are some ideas to try.

- ☐ Set boundaries for phone use, acceptable volume for music, time when you shouldn't be disturbed, and so on, and don't be surprised if they are repeatedly crossed. Just keep setting the boundary.

- ☐ Be as philosophical and flexible as you can about what you can achieve. Identify the things that you can let go and those you must do.

- ☐ Make the most of times when they are sleeping in (with any luck till early afternoon), out with friends and at school or college.

☐ Accept that you can't wear a business hat and a mother hat at the same time and find ways to cut down the emotional content of your interaction.

A Massage Therapist's Story

'My mother's antennae get tweaked when my son's around,' says Diane, who runs her practice from home, 'so I take my case notes and go off in the car to somewhere quiet with a nice view. I put on some classical music and write up my notes. Or I'll take a book and have a coffee in a café while I'm reading up on something.' She has also found that emailing or ringing her son when they are both at home means the communication is received differently: 'Ringing him on the mobile works better than banging on the wall.'

☐ Have a separate phone line put in and keep it out of bounds to save rows over phone use.

☐ 'Errands are good,' says Caroline. 'Send them off to walk the dog or go shopping so you can guarantee some peace and quiet for a while. You can also appeal to their mercenary side by paying them to do some small jobs.'

☐ Involve them in your business if possible, and let other people demonstrate the way to be professional. With luck they will acquire skills for the future.

Coping with customers in your home

In Chapter 4 we dealt with the issue of whether or not you should have meetings at home. For some homeworkers, there is no question about it as they live 'over the shop' and their clients and customers are paying to come into their home. Added to the issues of finding a way of working happily together and switching off when not attending to their customers, the next three couples also had to learn to cope with strangers being in their personal space. This is their experience in their own words.

The Cafe Proprietors' Story

'You've got to have a good relationship as working together can put a strain on it,' says Roger. Susannah and I enjoy each others' company and it was nice to work with her, although we didn't always agree.

I have a more rigid line between work and relaxation, what I consider my time, so I would have liked to stop serving cooked food at 4.40 p.m. (the café closed at 5 p.m.) to give us time to clear up. Susannah's view is that she doesn't do anything she doesn't enjoy, so for her there's not such a distinction between work and leisure.

149

I found that there's an element of performance in serving people and you find yourself playing up to the regulars and exaggerating aspects of your personality they seem to enjoy. I was the cantankerous one, banging pots about in the kitchen.

We enjoyed the unexpected, the element of surprise and the different interactions. We met some interesting people and as newcomers to the area, it was a good way to network quickly. People who liked the place tended to be people we felt comfortable with.

Our only loo was in our house, but it felt mean not to let people use it. I did feel a bit ambivalent about letting people into our space but mostly people respected it. I did used to lock the upstairs doors, though, as much as anything because I know how nosy people can be.'

At least a café closes in the evening and the customers leave. The owners of bed and breakfast accommodation don't have that luxury. If you feel your home is being invaded by work calls and emails, just try having clients who stay the night and expect a cooked breakfast the next morning!

The B&B Owners' Story

Tom and Penny have some guest accommodation in the house where they themselves live and some accommodation in a separate annex. Although they have been in the bed and breakfast trade for many years, they still can't switch off completely if there are people staying in the house: 'We relax more when there are no guests in the house – it has a totally different feel. When there are guests here I sleep with one ear open and leap out of bed if I hear noises.

We have learnt to circumnavigate one another if we have differences, as with guests about, rows are out of the question! Fortunately we have other interests we feel more strongly about than burning the sausages! We are both introverts and quiet people. A more extrovert couple would need to express themselves differently.

You have to understand yourself, your psychology and what your body needs, so you can get out and use your energy to reduce stress.'

Jane and Peter have a clever solution to maintaining their privacy while running a B&B – they live in one terraced house and accommodate their guests next door. But the doorbell, fire alarm and guests' bell are all connected to their home, so they are never off duty.

The Story of the B&B Next Door

'We never switch off,' says Jane. *'It's the responsibility of having people on our premises. We've had people become ill in the middle of the night and had to call the doctor or the ambulance. You become intertwined in other people's lives. Whatever befalls our guests tends to have a knock-on effect and befall us too. You never know what's going to come up and everyone is so different.*

The trouble with running your own business is that you're so intent on having a good business that you put yourself last. In the past we've blocked out time off but then a good booking's come up and we've scrubbed the time off. You make resolutions about going out for a meal every two weeks, but that evening guests will arrive late and the meal doesn't happen. It's easily said but so hard to do. Putting yourself last is OK short term but it doesn't work long term.'

Resources

☐ Family and friends who live locally and will help out with childcare.

☐ www.nhsdirect.nhs.uk
Use the self-help guide to identify your symptoms and medical conditions and get advice on treatment.

☐ www.andybritnell.co.uk
Our training and coaching website, where you can order a personality profile and a one-to-one coaching session.

☐ *The E Myth Revisited – Why Most Small Businesses Don't Work and What to Do About It* by Michael Gerber. Harper Collins, 1994.
Michael Gerber has distilled his experiences of helping American small businesses into this readable book. One of his main themes is the importance of allocating roles at the start of a business, which allows for efficient growth if needed.

☐ www.daycaretrust.org.uk
This national childcare campaign works to promote high quality, affordable childcare throughout the country.

☐ www.childcarelink.gov.uk
A source of national and local childcare information.

☐ www.workingfamilies.org.uk
Working Families helps working parents and carers and employers to achieve a balance between home and work responsibilities.

9

WHAT IF THERE'S A CRISIS?

An important part of the companionship of office life is the constant presence of fellow workers who can give you advice, guidance and a sympathetic ear when things aren't going well. That ready supply of advice becomes less accessible when you work from home and you may find yourself having to deal with all kinds of circumstances using your own resources.

This chapter covers:

1. The kind of challenges that might crop up for even the best organised homeworker, relating to money, family, technology, other people, bad luck, getting stuck, and running out of time. Plus the upheaval that an unmissable opportunity can bring.

2. A pick-and-mix of suggestions designed to make you feel better and tackle any setbacks effectively while keeping your cool.

What could go wrong?

Sometimes I have felt as though I am the only one who has to deal with challenges and setbacks at work and that other people just sail through smooth waters, gathering success and accolades as they go. The tendency of people in business to put a gloss on things and not talk about problems for fear of being thought less than successful only adds to this feeling of isolation. Business books and courses concentrate on explaining how to do things properly and tend not to mention the possibility of mistakes. (With the honourable exception of *The Small Business Start-up Workbook* by Cheryl Rickman recommended in the Resources section of Chapter 4, which includes interviews with household names about the blunders they have made and what it taught them.)

The feeling that you are somehow more unfortunate than others and unique in being cursed with difficulties can block you from thinking clearly about your situation and finding creative ways to improve it. Everyone has to deal with problems of varying magnitude all the time, and it is better to regard glitches as a normal part of everyday life than to see them as catastrophes that afflict only you. What follows is a list of the kind of challenges that can arise for any homeworker, in the hope that by being aired openly they will become less threatening. When you have finished reading about these potential hitches, keep on reading the next section of suggested solutions so you emerge feeling positive and confident that you are able to cope with anything that working from home might throw at you.

Financial worries

Most of us rely on our salaries to keep ourselves and our families afloat, and so financial worries can be the most profound and debilitating of all. This is true both for employed people anxious about keeping their jobs in a difficult economic climate and the self-employed competing in a market constantly looking to cut costs.

Money worries can make you feel desperate to keep earning at your current or a higher rate, and desperation can undermine your performance and actually reduce your chances of success at work. They can crop up in a variety of ways.

LOSING YOUR JOB OR THE WORK YOU DO ON CONTRACT

This is a worry that more and more people are having to learn to live with and that's really all you can hope to do. When I ran my cleaning business I was constantly aware that there were many competitors in the industry, nearly all of whom would be willing to do the job for less than I was charging. From time to time I would find flyers on doormats advertising cleaning services and feel anxious that my clients would be tempted to take their business elsewhere. It took a while, but eventually I realised that the possibility of losing business would always be there, and that all I could realistically do about it was to do the best job I could, maintain a good relationship with my clients and hope for the best. And that's all any of us can do. Worrying about possible future scenarios only makes you less effective.

NOT MAKING A PROFIT

It's a tired old cliché yet all too true that change is happening faster and faster. One of the side effects of constant change is that you have to keep your eye on the ball to make sure that your work continues to be profitable. Many industries are driving down costs by sending work to be done abroad, automating tasks that used to be done by hand or using large companies who attract economies of scale and can undercut smaller operators. The result is that the rate you are offered for a job, far from increasing in line with inflation, may be less than it was before. It's not pleasant to realise your lucrative niche no longer pays so well.

NOT GETTING THE JOB OR CONTRACT

As soon as you decide to apply for a new job or tender for a piece of work, your mind sets to work, not only preparing your application or bid but also imagining the accolades you'd receive, how getting the job would affect your life, and how your lifestyle would improve because of the extra income. That's a big investment of time, effort and emotion and to have it come to nothing can be a big blow.

Family and domestic emergencies

When you're working from home, anything that happens in the home or to anyone who lives with you has the capacity to impinge on your work routine. You can't dash out of the door in the morning and forget about home life until work is over for the day. These are the kind of things that might occur.

ILLNESS OR ACCIDENTS

Illness or accidents are probably the most distressing challenges you're likely to encounter while working from home. Being on hand, you are the one that is most likely to have to deal with them, whether that means rushing a child to the casualty department or interrupting your work to make drinks and snacks for a bed-bound family member.

And, of course, illness and accidents can also happen to you, but in these circumstances working from home can be an advantage. As you recover, you don't have to struggle to work feeling terrible, you can just pace yourself to work when you feel like it and take breaks when you get tired. (But be careful to keep a healthy line between work commitments and your own fitness, as discussed in Chapter 8.)

HOUSEHOLD EMERGENCIES

By household emergencies I mean the irritating and disruptive glitches that happen in any household. The boiler packs up on the coldest day of the winter leaving you shivering and cross, or a thunderstorm takes out your power supply, effectively cutting you off from the world and making it impossible to work.

MOVING HOUSE

Moving house is not a crisis in the sense that it suddenly hits you out of the blue; on the contrary, it might take months to achieve. But since your home is your workplace as well as where you lay your head, a house move is especially disruptive for homeworkers. Firstly there's the extra tidying and housework to be done to keep the place looking good for prospective purchasers, then there's all the packing up, including your workspace – and it's amazing how much stuff, and heavy stuff at that, is disgorged from a filing cabinet. Not to mention the disruption to work caused by the day of the move and then getting yourself back in working order at the other end. Friends warned me before our recent move that they had had problems with getting new phone lines but it was still an unpleasant shock to have to wait two weeks for the phone and almost a month for broadband.

ITglitches

Communications are key to homeworkers and so breakdowns can throw your working routine into turmoil. We are all dependent on technology these days to a greater or lesser degree and when it lets us down it can be difficult to achieve anything related to our usual routine.

WHEN THE TECHNOLOGY BREAKS DOWN

There are all sorts of reasons why technology can let you down and sometimes they are completely out of your control. In my case it was due to a frustrating series of delays and hitches in the order process used by the telecommunications company. Margaret had a panicky time when her computer, hitherto reliable, went into a terminal crash and she faced the possibility of losing hours of work.

A Publisher's Story

Nikki and Giles run their publishing company from their house in the country, and the wires that provide their internet connection have to cross fields and woodland. When the wires needed replacing recently, it was a major job that took BT several weeks to complete and for most of that time the business was without access to the internet: 'We were unable to send or receive emails from authors, editors and designers, and had no access to our daily sales reports, so we felt very cut off. As orders go direct to our distributors, we didn't lose any sales as far as we know, but it's impossible to know if we missed any opportunities through emails being lost. It was very inconvenient and stressful as we had to find different ways of doing things and all in a tight period of time to meet deadlines.'

WHEN YOUR IT KNOWLEDGE RUNS OUT

Many of us have acquired our knowledge of computers by picking it up as we go along, gleaning odd bits of information from colleagues when required and generally hoping for the best. When you need a bit more information or there's an unexpected glitch, a tiny detail can bring you to a grinding, frustrating halt.

People problems

Whatever your line of work, you are bound to have at least a few people you are in contact with and who have some effect on how you work or how good your output is. They might be your colleagues in head office, the stationery shop that supplies your paper or the people who work for you directly or on contract. In any human relationship, even with the best of intentions on both sides, there is the possibility of misunderstandings and sometimes people may simply let you down.

Ringing In Sick

❝ I used to dread the phone ringing at lunchtime, as this was the time cleaners were most likely to ring in sick. My niche market was professional offices that paid a premium to receive a top quality service and there was no question of a clean being skipped or skimped just because someone had a cold. My other cleaners would have to be asked to do some extra time or in the worst case scenario, I would have to do the clean myself, and with an already busy routine of checking offices and replenishing supplies, that meant a lot of disruption and a lot of work. At my worst times I felt at the mercy of my part-time staff and the vagaries of their lives. ❞

Bad luck

Some people regard themselves as lucky, some as unlucky and some don't believe in such a thing as luck at all. Deepak Chopra says that good luck is when preparedness and opportunity come together, which is an interesting take on the subject. By his definition, presumably 'bad luck' would mean a lack of preparation or lack of a genuine opportunity.

Whatever your feelings about luck, from time to time we all experience misfortunes that seem to come out of the blue. Things like car accidents, items disappearing in the post, the cancellation of a train or plane on the way to an appointment, annoying and inexplicable little quirks that can have a significant impact on how events turn out.

Getting stuck

We all run into brick walls with our work from time to time, regardless of where we work, but when you work from home you have to rely on your own ingenuity to generate fresh inspiration or find help. Before you can do that it's helpful to identify why you've run out of steam. Is it because you have been following the same old routine for too long, because you don't have the required expertise or because you need a break?

Running out of time

One of the most sickening feelings is the realisation that you are running out of time to complete a project and might have to deliver it late. It could be that you didn't allow yourself enough time to begin with or you've allowed your time and concentration to be deflected onto other matters.

A golden opportunity

To end this section on a happier note, it's important to remember that by no means all crises are unpleasant. For instance, you might get a call out of the blue offering you a lot of work, which you want to take on, but which will cause all kinds of upheaval. You might need to reorganise your current workload and clients, convince your family of the benefits of the new job and persuade them to help you out with the domestic duties, arrange travel and accommodation, liaise with others or take on staff. Deciding to go for such opportunities is exciting and scary at the same time, as you push out of your comfort zone and take on new responsibilities.

Cold Sweat and Hot Coffee

❛I remember being over the moon when I was asked to take on my biggest cleaning contract, which involved recruiting five staff to work every week-night. One day I was sitting at the kitchen table with a cup of coffee in the thick of organising interviews, buying new equipment and planning cleaning schedules when a horrible thought popped into my head – 'What if this all goes utterly wrong and I can't do what I've promised to deliver?' I remember literally breaking out into a cold sweat as the possibility of failure hit me for the first time. It gradually receded as I thought of ways to cope with all the disaster scenarios my imagination had immediately produced.❜

Ways to manage crises while keeping your head

This section is about getting over your own cold sweat moments as quickly as possible. Dealing with obstacles makes you more creative and better at coping with future challenges. In fact people are paid to solve problems, and the bigger the problem you can solve, the more you are likely to be paid. Here are some suggestions for viewing the situation in the best possible light, picking yourself up, and moving on, with any luck wiser and more resourceful than before.

Get away from the problem

Getting away from the problem is my favourite solution to all kinds of difficulties, as long as you don't use it as an excuse for procrastination. Don't keep banging your head against that brick wall – get away and find stimulation elsewhere. You'll be amazed at how ideas and solutions come out of nowhere if you just give your conscious mind a rest.

TRUST YOUR INSTINCTS

Don't force yourself to work when you don't feel like it. We have been heavily conditioned to believe every minute must be spent doing something productive, and productive usually means work related. It can be hard to break the habit of feeling guilty if you're not working all day, but freedom is one of the major advantages of working from home, so practise listening to your instinct about what to do at any given time. Many times I have hung fire on a particular element of work, not really understanding why, only to have a vital piece of information turn up that makes it easier to complete.

A Story of Intuition

❝ *Our house was on the market and in the middle of writing this book we received an offer, which we accepted. Somehow it felt far more constructive to clear out cupboards and prepare for the move than to continue with the book, although I did have occasional pangs of guilt. My instincts were vindicated when our purchasers suddenly announced they wanted a quick exchange of contracts, followed by completion within ten days. We were able to go along with their request and get the sale resolved, whereas if I'd stuck to writing the book for that time, it would have been impossible and in these uncertain times we might have lost the sale.* ❞

DO SOMETHING ELSE

Do something completely different, however bizarre or mundane. I find cleaning the bath gets my imagination fired up. A few minutes earlier I could have been sitting staring blankly at the computer screen with not an idea in my head, but as soon as I've got those rubber gloves on and the cream cleaner in hand, the brain cells start firing and I have to stop and write down all the thoughts that stream out of nowhere. Veronica used to be a coach in London and found that invariably she got her best ideas in Starbucks.

A Farmer's Story

John is a farmer who has diversified into making steel gates and railings, so as well as checking and harvesting his crops and the many tasks required to keep the farm going, he has a different outlet for his creativity. 'I have three benches in my workshop,' he says, 'because I have three jobs on the go. When I get tired of one, I drop it and move onto another, then come back later.'

TAKE YOUR WORK SOMEWHERE DIFFERENT

No matter how efficient and comfortable your workspace, sometimes it can get stale and that's when a change of scene can help. Move onto the kitchen table or sit by a window with a different view. If the weather's good, take your work outside.

If it's people and life you're missing, find out if the local library offers free internet access or wi-fi. You can find wi-fi at cafes in quite small towns, although all but the larger chains tend to charge. Have a look at Chapter 4 for more alternatives to working at home.

> **Just a thought:**
> If you get out of your box, you'll start to think outside the box.

SLEEP ON IT

A time-honoured solution to all kinds of difficulties, and a very good one. It's also the perfect excuse for an afternoon nap (see Chapter 5).

TAKE THE DAY OFF

Again this means going against the grain and trusting that something good will come out of it. I always find that a day in a different environment, whether it be walking in the country, wandering through galleries or meeting up with friends for lunch, gives me a boost of extra energy and sends me back to my desk feeling fired up for the task ahead instead of drained and anxious.

We have noticed many times that when we're stuck and nothing seems to help, if we go out for the day and forget about things, we get a call or email about work. Being able to relax seems to move things on.

GO OUT AND NETWORK

Meeting new people will recharge your batteries and you might just pick up a crucial piece of information. Have a look at Chapter 7 for some detailed information on how to get the best from networking.

EXERCISE THE BLUES AWAY

Now that she works from home, Sue goes to three exercise classes a week as a way of getting out of the house and working off her frustrations. Exercise is a good way of drawing the line between work and relaxation time (see Chapters 5 and 8 for more ideas).

HAVE A HOLIDAY

It doesn't have to be anywhere exotic, it doesn't even have to be abroad. The important thing is that you experience a different environment, so if you live in the country, a city break is good and vice versa. Somehow the change of place opens you up to new ways of being and doing things, even if you're in the same culture. It can stimulate new ideas and get you going on things you were totally stuck on.

Have a plan

Situations sometimes crop up without warning and knock us for six, but often it's possible to predict a potential problem and have a plan already organised to minimise the disruption. If you think it through when your life is going smoothly, you can swiftly put your plan into action when everything's turned upside-down, so do your own risk assessment on how likely it is an emergency will happen and different ways of coping if it does.

IT CONTINGENCY PLANS

Anything relating to office technology is a prime example of this kind of contingency planning. Office equipment seems to know when it is most required and break down at precisely that moment, so think of as many potential solutions as possible, which might include the following.

☐ Build a good relationship with a computer engineer.

☐ Carry out regular housekeeping on your computer to make the programs run faster.

☐ Protect your computer against viruses and hackers.

☐ Keep business and personal computers separate, especially if you have children. Free software can cause crashes and bring in bugs.

☐ Get your data backed-up off-site every evening.

☐ Ask an IT-literate family member to help out with occasional problems.

☐ Buy a broadband dongle.

☐ Research local places that offer free internet access e.g. coffee shops, the library, workhubs (see Chapter 4), a neighbour's wireless network.

☐ Keep good stocks of paper and ink cartridges, maybe a spare keyboard (you can get them for less than £10).

☐ Take your phone charger with you so you never run out of battery power.

PEOPLE CONTINGENCY PLANS

It's relatively easy to plan for mishaps involving technology, but those involving people tend to be a bit more tricky. Ask yourself what you would do if a child was sick – would there be anyone available to look after them if you had appointments to keep or would you have to postpone your meetings? Setting up a 'favour swaps' arrangement now will pay dividends in an emergency – Chapter 8 covers the art of working from home while looking after children.

HAVE SOME EXPERTISE TO HAND

A setback is easier to deal with if there's someone already in place you can call on for support. Your boss or your colleagues might be able to guide you, or you could look for a specialist.

Mentors

A mentor is someone you like and trust who has already trodden the path you are on, and can support you not only by encouragement but also by giving you access to their own network. Large employers often provide a formal mentoring scheme, or you can simply ask someone you respect to meet for lunch on a regular basis. People are usually flattered to be asked and willing to help as long as they are clear on how much time they will need to commit.

Coaches

Whereas mentors help over a long period of time, a coach is more likely to help you to deal with a specific goal over a shorter time – to get a promotion or gear your business up a notch, for example. Working with someone who knows the right questions to ask when the going gets tough helps you to achieve more than you can on your own. You might also like to refer to the section in Chapter 3 on useful people to know when you're setting up in business.

Just a thought:
You don't necessarily have to work hard on improving your weaknesses. Just concentrate on making your strengths, the things you naturally do well, even better and let someone else deal with anything you find a struggle.

Courses

If you are employed, your employer probably keeps you up to date with the latest skills required to do your job properly. For those who are self-employed, it's important not to be so blinkered by the need to get the job done that you get left behind. Training courses can seem prohibitively expensive and time-consuming, but like networking they often have many unforeseen benefits in terms of improving your morale and generating ideas. Free and subsidised training is available across many disciplines – see Resources at the end of the chapter to find out where to start looking.

Informal help

Knowledge and expertise doesn't have to come in the form of a structured training course, nor does it have to cost anything. Your best source of IT advice may well be your own or someone else's teenager.

For ongoing moral support and a chance to get out of the house, regular meetings with a friend in the same line of business can be a life-saver. Just as professional counsellors are obliged to regularly see a supervisor who listens to their concerns about clients and advises on dealing with tricky cases, a sympathetic ear and a chance to share worries can make the difference between being overwhelmed and staying positive. Without weekly meetings with a writer friend who was going through the same doubts and difficulties, I don't expect this book would have found a publisher, much less been written.

Put it in perspective

What has just happened probably seems like a total catastrophe right now, but will it still seem that way in ten years, two years, or even next month? In fact you'll probably have forgotten about many of your 'disasters' in a couple of years' time. Taking the long view will spare you a lot of stress.

Or it can help for you to step back and put the event in the context of your work and your life as a whole. Sue puts her worries about her dependence on the internet into perspective by remembering that by working from home she is saving herself two hours a day in commuting time.

A Psychologist's Story

Susan often works on a contract basis for large companies that can take several months to pay her: 'Sometimes I go months without any money coming in, so to reassure myself, I add up all the hours I've worked and calculate how much that's worth. I tell myself it's just a matter of time, that in the end it will come in, and it does.'

Use a fallow period constructively

It might be that your electricity has gone off during a storm, your phone line has been cut off or your computer has crashed, leaving you unable to continue work. It's a strangely discombobulating feeling, being disconnected from the web, but there is bound to be something you can do to fill the time until normal service is resumed. What about all that filing you never get round to? The people you have been meaning to phone? The office reorganisation you've been wanting to try out if only you had the time? A pause in normal working may just give you the opportunity to improve your systems and workspace so that you are more efficient when you get back to work.

When you are self-employed it is possible there will be times when nobody responds to your phone calls or replies to your emails, when arrangements are broken and you feel like a twenty-first-century business leper. If for some reason you've been temporarily spat out of the hungry jaws of commerce, use the time by networking or clearing out your filing cabinet. It won't be long before you're at everyone's beck and call again.

Choose your response

It is useful to learn to react to circumstances in a more positive way than you have been used to, especially if you have a large emotional investment in a particular issue or tend to be blown off course by small setbacks. There are always many different perspectives on any event, as you may have found when seeking sympathy from a friend for an experience you found difficult, only to find the sympathy unforthcoming because they took a different view.

A good way to get into the habit is to think back to experiences that initially seemed disastrous and how things actually turned out. You may have lost your job and felt your whole life was at an end, but subsequently found another job that suited you much better and had better prospects. The day after you were given notice you were in despair, but a few weeks or months later you were glad it had happened because without that push you would never have looked for another job. All you need to do is move forward to that positive emotion a little quicker. Maybe that member of staff who has upped and left at short notice will be replaced by someone who is much easier to work with and more talented. Maybe losing out on that contract means you are free to take on something else next week that opens up a whole new area.

A Trainer's Story

Not long ago my partner agreed to run a day's workshop for a local company and only two days later was offered a week's work abroad for that very week. He was fed up at the time because the week abroad would have paid many times his fee for the workshop. It crossed his mind to back out of the workshop, but that didn't feel right having made the commitment so he gritted his teeth and turned down the work abroad. Over a period of months the company he did the workshop for gave him more and more work, amounting in total to much more than the week abroad, which was a one-off with little chance of more work following.

Don't ask why but do ask for feedback

There's little point in wondering *why* a particular situation has occurred or why it has happened to *you*. There's never any satisfactory answer to that kind of question and you're just wasting valuable time and energy by focusing on it. However, it might be helpful to ask the people concerned for some feedback, for example why the contract was awarded to someone else. If you ask for this kind of feedback you must be prepared for an honest answer and to use the information to improve your chances next time. Taking it as a personal slight or as an indication you are not good enough is not going to help you.

You should also bear in mind that the person who took the decision may have moved on to other projects and be too busy to provide the kind of feedback you would find most useful. They may be unwilling to revisit their decision, so if not getting an answer would be even more hurtful, it may be better not to ask.

'You can't win 'em all'

The kind of remark that can be infuriating to hear, but nevertheless it's true. No matter how hard you work and how well you prepare, it's inevitable that you will fail from time to time. The success rate of direct mail campaigns can be as little as 2% but marketing companies don't stop sending out their promotional material because a huge proportion of it generates no sales. They simply assess the chances of success and plan accordingly.

A New Writer's Story

Jenny used to work for a charity, but gave it up to embark on a freelance writing career. She was worried about her apparent lack of success in getting assignments until it dawned on her that in her previous role her average success rate when writing bids was about 40%. In a paid job she was able to accept that only four out of ten of her attempts would actually pay off, but with her professional survival and self-esteem at stake, she was expecting a 100% success rate! By applying the 40% formula to her new career, she was able to relax and enjoy her work more, and surprise, surprise, started to get more commissions.

Even super-successful people have failures

We tend to get the impression from the media that certain individuals have the golden touch and always succeed no matter what they do. It's a short step from there to assuming that if we have failed at something, we obviously don't have that golden touch and we'll never succeed.

But according to Business Link, 20% of new businesses fail in the first year of trading and 50% in the first three years. So it stands to reason that even phenomenally successful people running a string of businesses have failures – in fact to achieve the successes they have, they must have had more failures than the rest of us!

Just a thought:
'Success comes from making enough mistakes.'

Remark attributed to Richard Branson

If you read the biographies and autobiographies of your own heroes, the people you believe have achieved great things, you'll find out how many setbacks and obstacles they had to overcome to finally achieve success.

There is no failure, only feedback

You might have heard this saying and found it either comforting or exasperating, depending on the circumstances. We are taught from an early age that success is good and failure is bad, to the point that many people don't want to risk trying something new in case they fail. Far better to think of life in terms of learning and development – if you will learn something by trying it out then it must be worth doing, even if you apparently 'fail'.

Share the pain

When you're in the midst of a crisis you understand the value of having a network of people you can ring for a good old moan and a consoling dose of sympathy. Just make sure you're not dumping on the same poor person all the time or that you only call when there's a problem, and have a look at Chapter 7 for more on the art of building a supportive network.

Susan's first year in business was a rocky ride but the pain was eased by being able to talk to other people who had been in the same situation: 'My partner is self-employed and understands how difficult it is when you start a business, so he was very helpful. I also spoke to other people in similar situations who reassured me that my situation was by no means unusual and I had to give it time.'

Just get on with it

I'm indebted for the title of this section to Annie, who works from home doing book-keeping and payroll, is studying for her accountancy exams, and has a baby, a ten-year-old, and a husband out at work all day. When asked how on earth she copes with all those conflicting demands on her time and energy, Annie simply replied 'Well, you just get on with it, don't you?' Her reply was echoed by several other homeworkers I spoke to soon afterwards.

Although impressed by Annie's unflappability, at first I found her answer a little unhelpful and mundane, hoping as I was for some special success formula I could impart. But then I realised that 'just get on with it' is as good a piece of advice as any to give to a homeworker. If you're not prepared to just get on with it in the face of challenges and setbacks, you're probably better off sticking with your job at the office.

It's also the case that the only way you figure out how to do something well is to...just get on with it. Theorising is fine but it won't actually achieve anything. Once you get started you can revise and fine tune, but getting on with it is the key.

Understand what's going on

Once you're over the initial shock and disappointment, think as objectively as you can about why you failed. Was it something you neglected to do, something out of your control – a change of policy or decision-maker – or just bad luck?

If you've come to a full stop with a project and can't seem to make it work, maybe you've gone off track somehow. Take a deep breath and a step back, stop worrying about it and think about what you are trying to achieve.

If you just can't get going on a project and you can't figure out quite why, if there seems to be a bigger blockage than simple procrastination, there may be something emotional going on, not necessarily relating to your working life. Talking to someone close may help you to uncover the underlying emotion and get you moving again.

You've got to laugh

And last but very far from least, it's true that sometimes you have to laugh because otherwise you'd cry. There's always got to be a funny side somewhere, no matter how bleak the situation at first appears, and learning to spot it will help you immensely. You can laugh at the ridiculousness of the situation, at other people's foibles, but especially at yourself. Laughter takes the stress out of the situation, and out of you, and leaves you in a better place to make a good decision and move on. I have a friend who can be relied upon to come up with an offbeat quip in the grimmest of situations and his humour has made me feel better on countless occasions.

Resources

- ☐ A friend with a dry sense of humour.

- ☐ There's nothing like a funny film to cheer you up. Humour is a personal thing, so rent DVDs of your favourite comedy series or try some of the classics like *The Pink Panther* films.

- ☐ www.getsafeonline.org
  Advice on using the internet safely on a site sponsored by the Government and leading businesses.

- ☐ www.learndirect.co.uk
  Find out about e-learning courses. Also check to see what is available from your local colleges and Business Link (www.businesslink.org.uk).

- ☐ www.happiness.co.uk
  The Happiness Project was founded by Robert Holden and has been featured on the BBC. Robert and his team run workshops and coaching programmes for blue chip companies and offer public events on achieving happiness and a positive attitude to life.

AFTERWORD

The great thing about working from home is that there's no need to behave as though you're still in an office. You can sleep during the day, have the dog sitting on your feet or break off from work to do a spot of weeding.

You are in charge and the way to make it work is to get to know yourself and what your brain and body need once they are freed from the constraints of nine-to-five life. There may be aspects of homeworking you don't like, but you have the liberty to make any changes you want to fit your temperament and circumstances better.

I have provided tips and ideas you may find useful but I don't believe there are any rules or clever formulas to ensure working-from-home success. By all means take note of my suggestions and the solutions found by the people featured here, but if it doesn't work for you, don't hesitate to reject it and find something else that does work.

Working from home can be a lonely place and my hope is that reading this book will help other homeworkers to feel 'Oh, thank goodness, it's not just me that feels like that. Maybe I'm not going mad, after all.' If you have enjoyed the book, you may also like to visit my website www.workfromhomewisdom.com

Good luck on your homeworking journey – there may not be a destination, but I hope you find the trip is worthwhile.

INDEX

professional association, 57

questionnaire
  are you ready for homeworking yet?,
    13
  are you suited to homeworking?, 32

reactive type, 32
re-energisers, 138
relating to people, 28
running expenses, 70

saying thank you, to different types,
  28, 107
self-employment, 47
self-motivation, 29
sensing type, 22
sockets, 70
sole trader, 47
solicitor, 56
space saving, in your workspace, 69
status, of your business, 47
structure, for your day, 84–8

suppliers, how they affect your
  professional image, 113
switching off, 135

tax, 49
technology, 4
teenagers, 148–9
thinking type, 23
'through-time' people, 31
timekeeping, 30, 105
time management, 88–9
time wasters, avoiding, 89

VAT, 49
visual type, 26

work/life balance, 5
work miles, 7
workhubs, 78
workspace
  improving, 63–76
  legalities, 64
  setting up, 63–76

Starting and Running A Coaching Business
Aryanne Oade

This book guides you through a comprehensive, practical and personalised process as you negotiate the pitfalls and reap the rewards of working alone, selling and marketing your business and taking sole responsibility for decision-making and problem-solving. It will help you establish and develop your coaching practice by identifying how you will handle each of ten key aspects of your business. You will discover how to define your coaching offer; find and sell your services to potential clients; handle your relationships with your clients; manage your business's finances; manage yourself and your ethical responsibilities; stay on top of your ongoing professional development; and much more.

ISBN 978-1-84528-332-2

How To Start and Run an Internet Business
Carol Ann Strange

'An excellent definitive guide.' – *Jobs & Careers*

This book will guide you through the process of establishing a profitable online venture and steer you towards success. You'll learn how to generate online income; create a reliable and appealing virtual shop window; optimise your web venture for growth; generate more profit from affiliate schemes and other prospects and become a successful internet entrepreneur

ISBN 978-1-84528-356-8

Start a Business from Home
Paul Power

This book will show you how to turn your passion and enthusiasm into a viable business. It is packed full of practical, down-to-earth advice based on the author's own, and other successful entrepreneurs', experience. Discover how you can easily research your ideas, start your own business at home, from little or nothing and market your business on a shoestring.

'His no-nonsense approach is inspirational.' – *Goodtimes*

ISBN 978-1-84528-301-8

How To Start and Run a Petsitting Business

Fiona Mckenzie

'An absolutely MUST HAVE for anyone that is starting up their own business. The book covers everything you need to know from a person who has gone through it themselves, and is written in a humorous helpful way. A book you will find essential when you are setting up and also to keep to refer to over the years once your business is up and running.' – Reader review

ISBN 978-1-84528-289-9

Start & Run a Successful Cleaning Business

Robert Gordon

This book will give you insider knowledge of the world of office and domestic cleaning and provide you with all the practical tools you need to succeed in a competitive but rewarding industry.

ISBN 978-1-84528-284-4

Starting & Running a Greetings Card Business
Elizabeth White

'Tells the reader everything they need to know about building an exciting and profitable business.' – *Greetings Today*

This book takes you step by step through the process of starting and running a business with lots of useful practical advice to help you.

ISBN 978-1-84528-264-6

Running a Bed and Breakfast: A Landlady's Guide

Christabel Milner

'Plenty of advice on the realities of running a B&B and its day-to-day management.' – *Best*

'The perfect escape plan.' – *Brand New You*

'Milner is like the sensible aunt you never had, full of amusing tales and common sense.' – French Magazine

'Anecdotal and easy to read, but full of detailed practical advice and the important lessons that need to be learnt. Covers everything from understanding the realities of running a B&B to its day-day management.' – *Food and Catering*

'An absolute gem of a book, which I enjoyed reading very much. Very clear and precise as well as entertaining.' – The Landlord Law Blog

ISBN 978-1-84528-269-1

Starting and Running a Catering Business

Carol Godsmark

'Full of practical information for the novice caterer including up-to-date details on catering legislation, employment laws and sourcing supplies, amongst other topics.' – *Spice Business Magazine*

'If you have a desire to get into catering you should read this book.' – *Delicious*

ISBN 978-1-84528-260-0

Starting Your Own Childminding Business
Allison Lee

'This is the perfect book for someone to read right at the beginning stages of thinking of becoming a childminder, especially before getting the ball rolling on becoming registered, and a good read before the Ofsted pre registration visit.' – National Childminding Association

'Offers all the advice you need to launch this extremely rewarding career.' – Jobs & Careers, Newsquest Ltd

'This is an excellent, back to basics book, and a valuable guide for both new and established childminders.' – Hollyhocks Childcare

ISBN 978-1-84528-097-0

Start Your Own Gardening Business
Paul Power

'A remarkably practical and helpful guide. Every subject from your business plan to tax legislation is covered here in straightforward and encouraging terms making you realise just what is possible. A life-changing book.' – *Permaculture Magazine*

'A practical and informative guide for anyone wishing to set up a new business.' – Royal Horticultural Society

ISBN 978-1-84528 175-5

How To Books are available through all good bookshops, or you can order direct from us through Grantham Book Services.

Tel: +44 (0)1476 541080
Fax: +44 (0)1476 541061
Email: orders@gbs.tbs-ltd.co.uk

Or via our website

www.howtobooks.co.uk

To order via any of these methods please quote the title(s) of the book(s) and your credit card number together with its expiry date.

For further information about our books and catalogue, please contact:

How To Books
Spring Hill House
Spring Hill Road
Begbroke
Oxford OX5 1RX
Visit our web site at

www.howtobooks.co.uk

Or you can contact us by email at info@howtobooks.co.uk